W9-ABV-825

IDENTIFYING AND DOCUMENTING

A COMMUNITY PROBLEM

FOR A POLITICAL CAMPAIGN

Angie Timmons

Rosen
YA™

New York

Published in 2020 by The Rosen Publishing Group, Inc.
29 East 21st Street, New York, NY 10010

Library of Congress Cataloging-in-Publication Data

Names: Timmons, Angie, author.
Title: Identifying and documenting a community problem
for a political campaign / Angie Timmons.
Description: New York : Rosen Publishing, 2020 | Series: Be the change!
: political participation in your community | Includes bibliographical
references and index. | Audience: Grade 7 to 12.
Identifiers: LCCN 2019013273| ISBN 9781725340848
(library bound) | ISBN 9781725340831 (pbk.)
Subjects: LCSH: Political campaigns—Juvenile literature. | Political participation—
Juvenile literature. | Community organization—Juvenile literature.
Classification: LCC JF2112.C3 T54 2019 | DDC 324.7—dc23
LC record available at https://lccn.loc.gov/2019013273

Manufactured in the United States of America

CONTENTS

INTRODUCTION

On the afternoon of February 14, 2018, nineteen-year-old Nikolas Cruz paid a visit to his former high school, Marjory Stoneman Douglas High School in Parkland, Florida, armed with an AR-15 assault-style rifle. Cruz opened fire, killed fourteen students and three staff members, wounded fifteen other people, then snuck out of the school amidst the crowd of people fleeing for their lives. He was apprehended an hour later and eventually charged with seventeen counts of premeditated murder.

The Stoneman Douglas shooting was the worst high school shooting since the April 20, 1999, massacre at Columbine High School in Colorado, in which two twelfth graders killed twelve of their fellow students and one teacher before committing suicide in the school library. School shootings became an unfortunately common news headline in the years that followed Columbine. A February 14, 2018, *Washington Post* article reported that since 2000, more than 130 shootings had occurred at American elementary, middle, and high schools. More than fifty shootings had happened at colleges and universities.

Shortly after the shooting at Marjory Stoneman Douglas High School, a group of students who survived the shooting sprang into action. In the wake of the tragedy, they made use of the press attention to share

The March for Our Lives movement, which was started by survivors of a high school shooting, called attention to the issue of gun violence and the need for reform.

their stories and call for gun reform measures. Inspired by the students' bravery, supporters across the nation demonstrated outside of state houses, flooded elected officials with phone calls and letters, and staged school walkouts to demand tighter gun control laws.

On March 24, just one month and ten days after the shooting, the Stoneman Douglas survivors brought their demands for gun control legislation to Washington, DC, by organizing a huge demonstration called the March for Our Lives. Hundreds of thousands of supporters held satellite marches in cities around the world.

What began as a group of high school students protesting against gun violence turned into the activist organization March for Our Lives. The organization has developed a comprehensive policy agenda and its members actively pressure lawmakers to draft and adopt gun control measures. The founders of March for Our Lives stayed active and loud throughout 2018 and urged voters to pressure their elected officials on the issue of gun control, making it a key issue in the run-up to the midterm elections. On November 6, 2018, Democrats—most of whom openly supported gun reform measures during their campaigns—became the majority party in the US House of Representatives.

March for Our Lives is a powerful example of what can happen when young people identify a problem, document their experiences, and demand that political candidates and elected officials acknowledge and address the problem. While the future of gun control legislation in the United States is unclear, the Stoneman Douglas survivors reminded the public that important things can be accomplished when people work toward solving community problems. They showed that power lies within the will of the people and that elected representatives should remember that they work on behalf of the people they represent.

CHAPTER ONE

IDENTIFYING THE PROBLEMS IN YOUR COMMUNITY

Communities take all forms: families, schools, faith-based organizations, towns, regions, states, ethnic groups, the list goes on. You are part of several communities, whether you realize it or not.

"The idea of having a 'community' at all might feel foreign to you, whether you're living in your hometown or you change addresses with the seasons," wrote Jackie Bernstein in Bustle. "But even if you feel like your community is just an accident of where you were born, or the place where you attend school or work, it can be much more than that."

Nations are comprised of millions of communities, each with its own identity, culture, concerns, and needs. Like individual people, each community has its own problems. But in any given town, county, congressional district, and state, these individual communities occasionally come together for one unified purpose: electing public officials.

Communities are made up of people who have something in common. This could be where you live, how you identify, or what you believe in. Every community has its own needs.

WHAT'S SO INTERESTING ABOUT ELECTIONS?

Political elections are a vital part of a democracy. If that statement makes you feel like yawning, think about why that is and what you can do to change it! What pops into your mind when you think of the word "politics"? Maybe you imagine boring government stuff that older people are supposed to deal with. Maybe you remember a scandal involving a politician. You may imagine a government building full of men and women you've never heard of, bickering over complicated issues. Considering some of these common

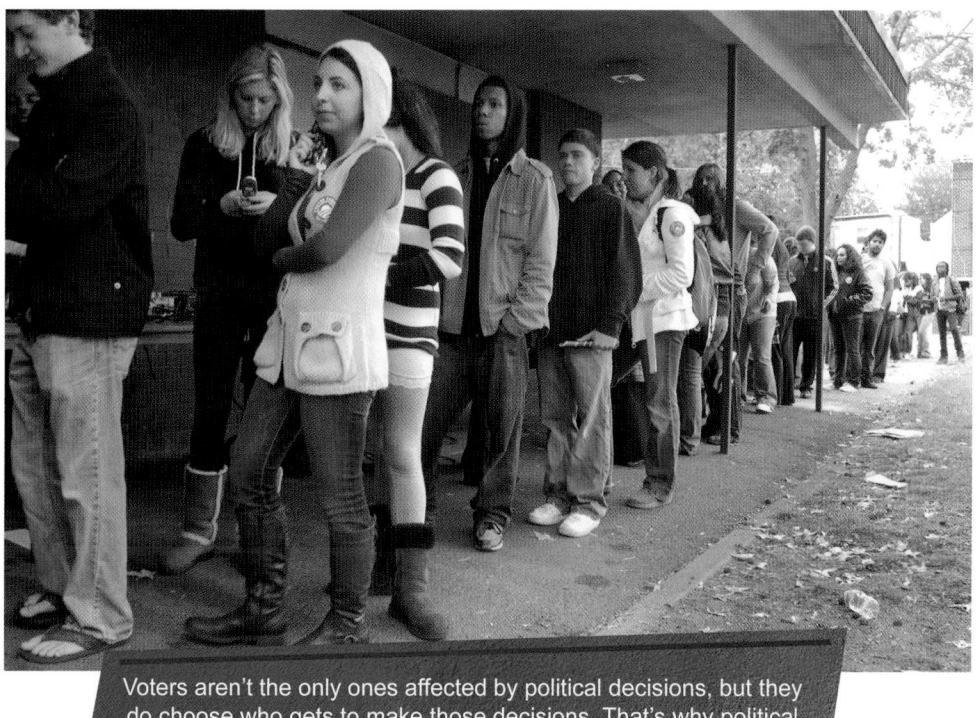

Voters aren't the only ones affected by political decisions, but they do choose who gets to make those decisions. That's why political participation is so important.

associations, you may wonder why politics gets so much attention.

Political elections get a lot of attention because their outcomes directly affect everyone. Elections give voters the chance to make choices that determine everything from who will make decisions about your education to who will lead the nation for the next four years. For many people, elections are the only time they get to make their voices heard on issues they care about, such as the environment, education, or health care. Even if you aren't yet old enough to vote, elections are a great way to learn about politicians, candidates, and problems or issues that impact you and your future.

DECISION MAKERS

The United States is a republic in which the power is held by the people and the representatives (sometimes called elected officials or lawmakers) elected by the people. The highest elected office in the land is president, but many different elected officials on local, state, and federal levels make decisions that impact people's lives.

Locally, most towns have an elected mayor and city council. These representatives vote on matters such as how much money city departments (like the police) get each year and on some taxation issues. Local school boards—either elected by voters or appointed by another authority, such as a mayor—make decisions related to education. Judges are often elected, and in some states, local sheriffs are elected.

On the state level, elected governors and elected legislatures meet in state capitals and work on laws specific to their state. Legislatures typically comprise senators and representatives who are elected by voters from their home districts.

Members of the US Congress (divided into the House of Representatives and the Senate) are elected by voters in their home states. Every state gets two senators, while the number of House representatives each state gets is based on the state's population.

Why does it matter who governs in your town, school district, or state? There are a few reasons. Most politics is local, meaning a lot of what happens in your life is decided on the local or state level. It also matters because local government is often a stepping-stone for people who aspire to higher elected offices. Many US senators, congresspeople, and presidents started in local or state government. The more good people are elected locally, the more good people are likely to be elected to higher levels of office in the future.

UNDERSTANDING CAMPAIGNS

Every year, some kind of election happens. Some of those elections are local, such as elections for mayor or school board, and some are special elections to fill an open seat on a local governing board or to vote on certain issues. Every two years, there are midterm elections, in which voters can elect state, local, and national representatives and other officeholders in the middle of the president's four-year term. Every four years, people vote for the president of the United States.

In the run-up to these elections, candidates run campaigns to try to win the support of their constituents. You may have seen people handing out campaign literature on the street or notice political signs posted in your neighbors' front yards. You may have even attended a political rally. These are all

Campaigns give candidates the opportunity to gain name recognition and share their political platforms before the election and to drum up support among voters.

examples of political campaigning, an often creative and intense process by which candidates for public office make their case to voters. Campaigns can go on for months or even years, depending on the office a candidate is running for. They can get very heated and personal, especially when the race between two candidates is close.

Political campaigns provide a way for candidates to communicate with their constituents about their positions on various issues. They help candidates get to know the people and the communities they hope to represent, and they allow those people and communities to get to know the candidates. Voters depend on campaigns to figure out what decisions they'll make at the voting booth on Election Day. Candidates depend on campaigns not only to persuade voters to support them, but also to set themselves apart from other people running for office. One way they set themselves apart is in how they address community problems during their campaigns and how they propose solving those problems.

POLITICS STARTS WITH YOU

Consider something you want or consider a priority, such getting accepted onto a team or being admitted to your college of choice. Now consider some problems you might be worried about: grades, a fight with a friend, a date, bullying, paying for college, or getting along with your parents.

How does it feel to think that you might not get the things you want? How does it feel to wonder if the problems you're worried about will ever be resolved?

WHAT IS A COMMUNITY PROBLEM?

There's a long list of issues that qualify as community problems. Some are obvious because they affect most communities and are easily recognizable. These are things like violence, homelessness, poverty, economic recession, or inadequate transportation. Other community problems and their impacts can be harder to detect. These things may include racial discrimination, drug addiction, lack of health care, domestic violence, child or animal abuse, economic inequality, and environmental damage.

Your specific communities, such as your school, may face other problems not listed here. Think critically about this. What problems do you see or hear about? What bothers you? What would you like to see fixed? To identify a community problem, consider:

- how frequently it occurs
- how long it's been going on
- how many people it affects
- how severe it is
- if it creates inequality or denies people certain rights
- how people in the community view the problem.

Once a community problem has been identified, the next step is figuring out how it became a problem.

Usually, problems are symptoms of something else. For example, Nikolas Cruz exhibited symptoms indicating that he was capable of violence before the Stoneman Douglas High School shooting. He was isolated and angry (symptoms) after the death of his mother and after multiple schools couldn't help resolve his developmental and emotional issues (problem). He posted about violence and killing (symptoms) but was able to buy guns anyway (problem). If Cruz's peers and community

(CONTINUED ON THE NEXT PAGE)

(CONTINUED FROM THE PREVIOUS PAGE)

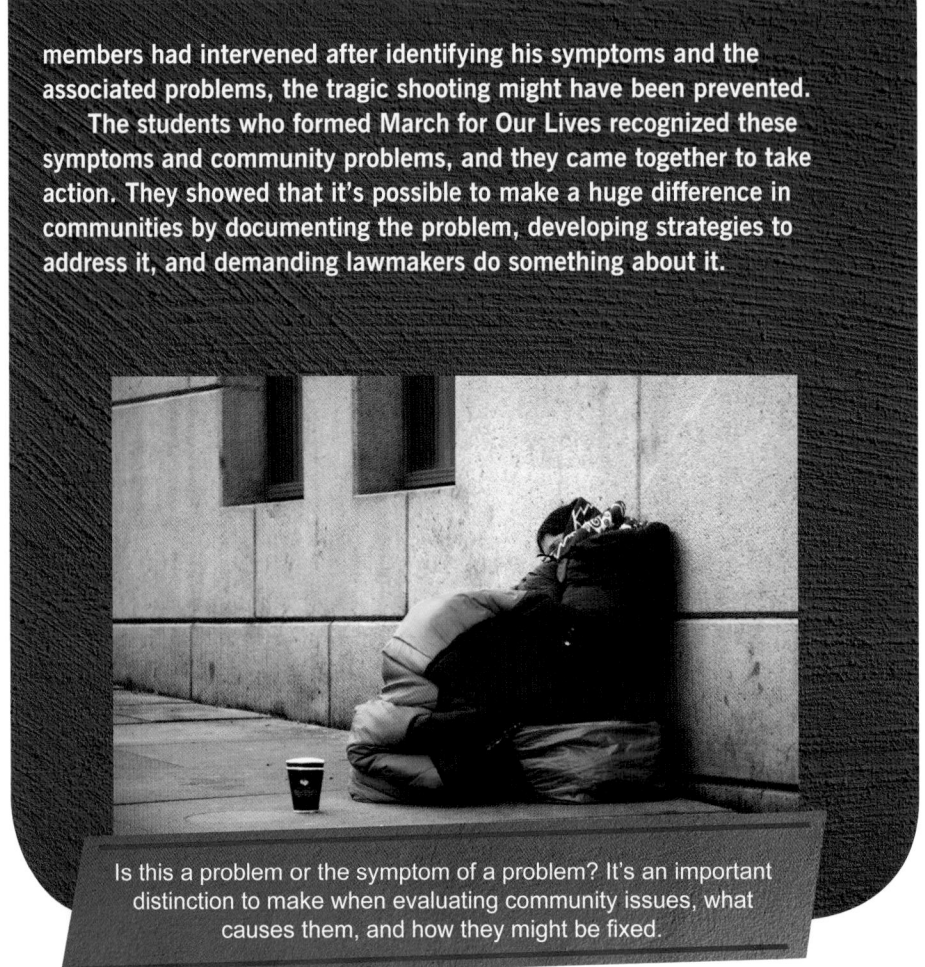

members had intervened after identifying his symptoms and the associated problems, the tragic shooting might have been prevented.

The students who formed March for Our Lives recognized these symptoms and community problems, and they came together to take action. They showed that it's possible to make a huge difference in communities by documenting the problem, developing strategies to address it, and demanding lawmakers do something about it.

Is this a problem or the symptom of a problem? It's an important distinction to make when evaluating community issues, what causes them, and how they might be fixed.

Chances are, you feel frustrated because so much of your life is in the hands of other people, like your parents, teachers, college admissions boards, or even classmates. Wouldn't it be nice to have the chance to have more say in the decisions that impact you? Or to have the chance to find people who not only share your concerns, but also want to fix them?

In the world of politics, elections give voters the opportunity to vote for people they hope will positively impact their lives and solve problems they're worried about. Campaigns give people the opportunity to share their priorities and concerns with candidates and find out what those candidates plan to do about them. On the campaign trail, candidates will learn about communities and their problems. This provides a valuable education for candidates because most of politics involves handling community problems. In fact, most legislation is reactive, meaning lawmakers enact laws in response to problems, rather than making laws as a preventive measure for a problem that hasn't happened yet.

During a campaign, political candidates should do all they can to become acquainted with the various needs of the communities they hope to represent.

Many young people don't think politics matters because they don't see much connection between their own personal concerns and what the government does. Some disregard politics because they're not old enough to vote. Gareth Morgans, a Houston-based political campaign adviser who's worked on fifteen campaigns, gave the following advice in an interview with the author:

> You might not be able to vote now, but the people that are voting now are making decisions that will impact you in your future: whether it's your family, education and training, future job opportunities, and quality of life … While you might not be able to vote now, you can make sure your voice is heard by the people voting now, and heard by the people they elect.

CHAPTER TWO

UNDERSTANDING THE COMMUNITY

In 1985, Barack Obama had recently graduated from Columbia University and was having trouble finding a job when he applied to work for the Developing Communities Project (DCP), an organization formed in 1984 to help people affected by widespread unemployment in Chicago. DCP was operated by community organizers—people who bring together community members to work toward common goals and solutions.

DCP was trying to bring together Chicago's historically divided white and black communities to work on employment solutions that would benefit everyone. Organizers at DCP believed that Obama's background and experiences as the son of a white American mother and a Kenyan father could help him bring together different communities. What they didn't know when they hired Obama was that this community organizing position was laying the foundation for his future presidential campaign.

COMMUNITY ORGANIZING: THE BEST EDUCATION

Before working with DCP, Obama had never really been forced to consider the role that his race played in his interactions with the communities he identified with. Working for DCP, however, he spent a lot of time interacting with black communities for the first time. He showed an ability to interact with and be accepted by people from a diverse range of communities. He also had an uncanny ability to convince different communities to set aside their differences and work together. This was the beginning of Obama's political journey.

Obama believed that feeling a sense of community and belonging could help people take an interest in politics and inspire them to get involved. Instead of staging protests to demand more jobs and economic opportunities (the way things had been done in Chicago for a long time), Obama brought together community leaders to work on the city's problems. For example, in an unprecedented collaborative achievement, Obama got the leaders of nearly all of Chicago's religious groups to meet and identify and strategize about community problems and solutions. In turn, those religious leaders got members of their faith communities to get involved. This resulted in thousands of people of diverse faiths, races, ethnicities, backgrounds, and political affiliations working together to solve community problems.

After three years with DCP, Obama went on to earn a law degree at Harvard University, get elected to the

President Barack Obama's journey to the highest office in the land began on a community level. This experience helped him inspire many communities and voters during his presidential campaign.

Illinois State Senate, and eventually, get elected to the US Senate. He became the Democratic nominee for president in the 2008 election and won, becoming the first black president of the United States. He served two terms. Obama has described his three years of community organizing with DCP as the best education he ever received and one of the main reasons he was a successful presidential candidate.

INSPIRING COMMUNITIES

As a presidential candidate, Obama electrified diverse segments of the electorate. His campaign rallies were widely attended by people from diverse backgrounds.

He spoke sincerely about his personal background and his work as a community organizer, showing a direct understanding of common problems, such as unemployment and lack of health insurance. Obama encouraged the black community, a historically underrepresented political community, to participate in the democratic process: the number of black voters in the 2008 presidential election jumped almost 10 percent compared to the 2004 presidential race between Republican George W. Bush and Democrat John Kerry.

Obama also inspired young people to participate in the political process: about half of all eligible voters between eighteen and twenty-nine voted in 2008 and 2012, with Obama winning most of their votes, according to Politico. This was a significant leap compared to the 1990s and early 2000s, when only about 40 percent of eligible young people voted.

Barack Obama's presidential campaign helped many people to stop seeing politics as a distant process that didn't involve them, but rather, as an exciting part of community life and something in which they could actively participate.

GETTING TO KNOW THE COMMUNITY

To be effective politicians, candidates need to prove they understand key community problems and present detailed plans to address those problems. Candidates identify community problems in a number of ways. To begin with, they're usually familiar with some

BETO O'ROURKE AND COMMUNITY ORGANIZING

In June 2018, US congressmember Beto O'Rourke, a Democrat from the Texas border town of El Paso, led hundreds of people in a march on the West Texas town of Tornillo, where about two hundred children had been detained after being separated from their parents when attempting to immigrate to or seek asylum in the United States. O'Rourke and his followers were protesting President Donald Trump's policy of separating children from their parents as a measure to prevent undocumented immigrants from entering the country.

At the time, O'Rourke was running for US Senate in a historically Republican state. He knew he needed some Republican voters to switch sides in order to win. Despite knowing the march could hurt his chances with those voters, O'Rourke rallied communities and marched anyway. In doing so, he used a tactic that many candidates fear: taking a very public and firm stance on a controversial issue—in this case, immigration policy. He used his campaign to draw attention to the issue and inspire action. It worked: in the months that followed, busloads of people descended on border towns to protest family separation. O'Rourke, who lost to

Beto O'Rourke used his 2018 Senate campaign to draw attention to controversial problems, like immigration enforcement, that need comprehensive and long-lasting solutions.

(CONTINUED ON THE NEXT PAGE)

(CONTINUED FROM THE PREVIOUS PAGE)

Republican senator Ted Cruz by only three points, sacrificed potential votes to urge communities to act on an important issue.

O'Rourke's Senate campaign drew many comparisons to Obama's youthful, community-centric style. He made an unprecedented effort to meet the people of all 254 Texas counties and unify them over key issues in one of the most intense Senate races in American history. Also, like Obama, many of O'Rourke's supporters were young people from diverse backgrounds who found his energy, passion, and commitment to change inspirational. And while he may have lost his Senate race, O'Rourke's campaign helped him to go from being a little-known congressmember to a national political superstar.

community problems because they are themselves part of the community. When Republican Angel Rivera, a longtime Indianapolis resident, ran for Indianapolis City-County Council in 2010, it was because he'd observed firsthand some critical issues that the city needed to address. "Crime and decaying infrastructure were at the top of my mind. Indianapolis was also getting distracted with less urgent issues," Rivera said in an interview with the author. "But the city could barely balance its budget and had great legacy costs that it faced in the future."

While campaigning, Rivera had to learn about other problems voters cared about, which were often different from the problems that had inspired him to run in the first place. He needed to prove he understood those problems and had plans to address them in addition to his key issues of crime and infrastructure. To do this, he hit the campaign trail and met people from the city's many communities. He then created specific campaign messaging to appeal to various voter communities, all of which cared about issues specific to their communities or had their own unique perspectives on citywide issues. Because he was running for an "at-large" council seat (meaning he'd represent all residents rather than residents within a specific district), Rivera had to appeal to basically everyone. "The urgency of certain issues changed from one group to the next." Rivera's campaign was successful and he was voted into office, where he served as city-county councilor from March 2010 to December 2011.

IDENTIFYING COMMUNITY PROBLEMS

Rivera's campaign is an example of an issues-driven campaign. In an issues-driven campaign, candidates recognize there may be community problems they're not very familiar with because they don't experience them personally. For example, a candidate from an upper middle class neighborhood might not have firsthand experience with the homeless problem in his or her town, but this person will still be responsible for addressing it if elected.

An issues-driven candidate does the legwork to identify as many community problems as possible while also getting to know the people in the district. Candidates might attend local civic meetings or meet with parents and teachers to learn about budget, safety, and educational issues. They may attend various religious services or events sponsored by diverse

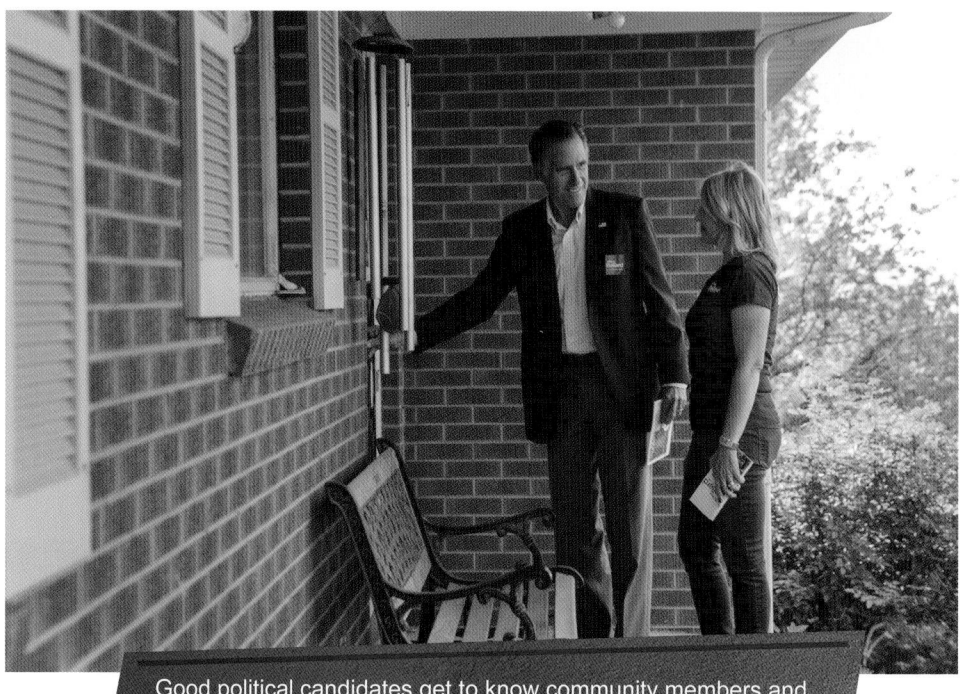

Good political candidates get to know community members and their concerns. They visit different neighborhoods, attend events, and start working on solutions to the problems they learn about.

ethnic groups to learn about the specific concerns of those communities. They might attend public events, where they can meet a lot of different people at once. Some candidates also use old-fashioned, yet effective, campaigning techniques such as knocking on doors or calling people to introduce themselves, share their ideas to address key issues, and learn more about what matters to the people they're talking to.

Through all these methods and more, candidates should develop a strong sense of the problems facing their communities and the steps voters want to see taken to address those problems. Candidates who take an issues-driven approach to campaigning often

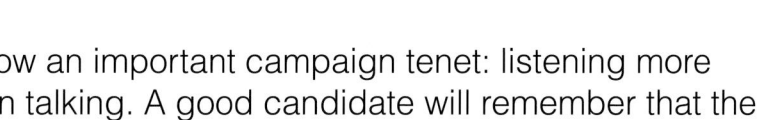

follow an important campaign tenet: listening more than talking. A good candidate will remember that the campaign is about the voter, not the candidate.

Candidates who fail to do this work usually make poor elected representatives. That's because elected officials are supposed to work on behalf of the people and the issues people care about, and they can't do that if they haven't made the effort to get to know the people they represent.

DOCUMENTING COMMUNITY PROBLEMS

While candidates are identifying community problems before and during their campaigns, they have to take an extra step: documenting what they learn. Well-funded or high-profile campaigns will usually have staff dedicated to researching problems, polling (surveying) the public to find out what matters to people, and compiling the data for the candidate's use in speeches, position statements, and debates. In smaller campaigns, the candidates themselves and their campaign teams will do this research and documentation through meeting or talking directly with members of the public. Most candidates will focus on a handful of community problems to address in their campaigns. Ideally, they'll get to know these problems very well and craft detailed plans to address them. They can use their research to show voters that these problems matter and require the action of dedicated elected representatives. Often, candidates will use their research and data to post position statements

Campaign literature is one way that candidates can document a problem and share their plans to address it. This can help raise awareness of problems and rally voters' support.

on their campaign websites, in press releases, and on campaign literature such as flyers. Candidates are increasingly using the internet to document community problems via social media posts in which they share statistics on problems and their ideas to solve them.

DEVELOPING A POLICY AGENDA

To develop a policy agenda, the Parkland students who formed March for Our Lives combined the evidence that someone like Cruz was capable of violence with the reality that, despite this evidence, he was still able to obtain guns. The organization laid out its policy agenda demanding additional legislation that could prevent the kind of gun violence its founders suffered.

Just like March for Our Lives, political candidates must develop policy agendas. These agendas are usually dictated by the problems that the candidates have identified and documented. The agendas of worthy candidates will show that they put the needs of their communities first by developing and proposing solid solutions to community problems.

CHAPTER THREE

ASSESSING A CANDIDATE

People run for elected office for many reasons. Some see political office as a stepping-stone or résumé builder for their careers. Some run for office because they come from a family of public servants. Some run for office to try to keep their political party in power. Almost all candidates, however, claim a desire to effect meaningful change and address issues as the inspiration to run for office. During campaigns, candidates focus on key issues—a handful of problems and proposed solutions to those problems that define their political agendas. Often, these issues will be a mix of issues that candidates know voters care about and issues the candidates themselves are passionate about. Together, these issues are the legs that hold up a candidate's campaign platform—an official set of goals designed to appeal to voters.

It's not enough for candidates to simply learn about, acknowledge, and document key issues, though. They also need to do the hard work of finding solutions for community problems. Their proposals for addressing key issues are the foundation of their campaigns, but how good are those proposals? How do you know if candidates will follow through on their proposals once elected? Do they genuinely care about the issue or are they just trying to get votes? Do they seem like they'll listen to constituents? Will they be open to working with members of the other party?

There are a number of ways to evaluate political candidates to assess their worthiness. It's crucial to pay attention to how well local or state elected officials represent the people who elected them.

Candidates focus on specific key issues that provide the foundation for their campaign platforms. These issues are generally problems in the community that need to be addressed by elected officials.

Otherwise, ineffectual or morally compromised leaders may continue to be elected to office. So how do you evaluate an elected official's performance?

EVALUATING YOUR REPRESENTATIVES

To start with, review elected officials' voting records alongside a list of their campaign donors. (You can get this information from websites such as votesmart .org and fec.gov. This information will also be useful when assessing incumbent candidates—candidates running for reelection.) If they seem to vote based on donors, political action committees (PACs), or special interest groups (which use money or power to pressure elected representatives to vote in certain ways), they're not voting on your behalf; they're voting to please the people who likely bankroll their reelection campaigns or offer other perks.

In 2018, March for Our Lives took a stand against the influence special interests groups have on politics after the group was repeatedly asked to endorse or support candidates running in the midterm elections. David Hogg, one of the group's founders, posted a powerful reminder for candidates and elected officials: "Don't call us asking for endorsements. The only thing we endorse is common sense policies. Don't call us asking for political donations. If you need money from special interest groups then you shouldn't be running. Sincerely, March For Our Lives."

Another way to assess elected officials is by looking for evidence of "party line" politics, wherein an elected official's legislative priorities and voting patterns are dictated by their political party affiliation (such as Republican or Democrat) rather than by what their constituents want. Because many elected offices don't have term limits, elected officials are often more focused on reelection than they are on legislation. Therefore, they seldom try to appeal to voters from outside their party, openly support the opinions of the opposite political party, or work with the opposing party because their reelection depends on keeping the support of their voting base and political party.

As a result, many members of the two major political parties have become uncompromising in their stances on key issues because their reelection depends on upholding their party's views. If elected officials consistently vote along party lines, they're probably

Good candidates and elected officials put aside party politics to propose or vote on legislation the way most of their constituents want them to—not the way their party dictates.

not putting in the hard work to find out what all their constituents want, regardless of party affiliation. They may even be unwilling to assess the merits of the opposing party's ideas or to pay attention to their own constituents' correspondence about upcoming legislative decisions because they've already decided to vote along party lines before the legislation even goes to a vote.

It is also possible to evaluate elected officials based on their voting records. If they're ineffectual legislators (meaning they write, sponsor, or involve themselves in few legislative bills), then they're not making the most of their ability to work on behalf of their constituents. If an elected official's legislative and voting records show an unwillingness to collaborate or compromise with elected officials from the opposite political party, they may not be doing a good job. Representatives' voting records should reflect whether they've reached across the aisle to work on legislation.

EVALUATING A CANDIDATE DURING A CAMPAIGN

Evaluating candidates and campaigns can be harder than evaluating elected officials. Unlike elected officials, who can be assessed through concrete evidence such as voting and donor records, candidates, especially first timers, can sweep voters off their feet with big promises, charisma, and slogans but may not have any concrete evidence to support these promises. These surface-level characteristics tend to dominate campaign materials, manipulate public perception, attract attention to the candidate rather than the issues, and allow candidates to avoid directly addressing anything that might lose them votes (such as taking a stand on controversial issues).

Campaigns can suddenly seem a lot more interesting when you consider whether candidates in your town or state are trying to pull a fast one on voters by using surface-level tactics. If you discern that a candidate is becoming popular by superficial means, it's kind of like finding out that a classmate might get into an Ivy League university by lying about his or her grade point average. When you consider that an undeserving candidate might actually get elected and affect your future, it makes sense that you would want to invest some time and energy to make sure you are

Those who are not old enough to vote can still make their voices heard by participating in community work or attending rallies for issues they care about.

voting for candidates because of their substance rather than their style.

CONSIDER THE ISSUES

What do you care about? The environment? Animals who need homes? Poverty? Money for college? What do you think an elected official should do about the things you care about? These are the first steps in deciding what you want in a candidate who might one day have the power to make laws that affect you and the things you care about. Knowing what issues you care about can also help you figure out which political party you identify with. Or perhaps you see yourself as an independent, someone who sees some good ideas on both sides. Envision what qualities your ideal leaders would have. Do you want them to be smart, sincere, passionate, or have a background in one of the issues you care about (such as environmental activism or helping the homeless)?

LEARN ABOUT THE CANDIDATES

Once you know what issues you care about and the leadership qualities you want in an elected official, consider those issues in the context of a campaign. Chances are, there is an election in the pipeline that you can study. Find out which candidates are running. A good resource for this is VOTE411.org, run by the nonpartisan group League of Women Voters (LWV).

Campaign adviser Gareth Morgans shared some easy places to start learning about candidates:

Every candidate running for office has a campaign website where they list the issues that concern them and why they're running. Visit each website, print out and review the issues, and make a list of questions that you think about as you study their agenda. Reach out to the campaign office, or better yet, attend a candidate forum and ask your questions directly to the candidate.

As you go, collect campaign literature, mailers, press reports, advertising, video or transcripts of campaign

Get to know the people running for office. Find out when candidates are holding forums or events near you so you can meet them, ask questions, and share your ideas.

speeches, and information about candidates' debates (which may be covered by the media or campaign headquarters may have video records). Once you've collected these materials, review them to find out where the candidates stand on issues you care about. Morgans had the following advice for this step:

> Always make sure to review and cross reference any facts the candidate may use, and always ensure the source material is from a legitimate organization. One of the best resources is your local (credible) newspaper or TV stations: have they screened the candidate and what questions did they ask? How did the candidates respond?

> The League of Women Voters (LWV) is also a good resource for information about candidates in local, state, and federal races.

ASSESS WHETHER THEY WILL BE GOOD LEADERS

Knowing whether candidates will make good elected officials is difficult. Both first-time and incumbent candidates can use campaigns to convince voters that things will be different if they're elected. How do you truly vet the leadership abilities of the people behind the campaign glitz?

First, investigate candidates' experience. Do they have professional backgrounds, advocacy experience, or a history of community involvement that has prepared them for the challenges of elected office?

BEWARE OF DISTORTION TECHNIQUES

All candidates are vying for public support. Many rely on traits that make them popular, like good public speaking skills or personal charisma, to create the appearance of worthiness rather than really addressing the issues. How can you see through this? Look for "distortion techniques" that campaigns employ to manipulate voters. Here's a list of common distortion techniques from the LWV:

- Name-calling or prejudicial attacks based on opponents' characteristics that have nothing to do with political ability, such as race or religion
- Starting or spreading rumors about an opponent without evidence of wrongdoing; just implying the opponent may be guilty of something is often damaging enough
- Guilt by association, wherein a candidate attacks an opponent based on the opponent's supporters, such as endorsements from advocacy groups or donors
- Catchwords used to elicit emotional responses instead of inform voters (such as "un-American")
- Blaming an opponent for something he or she couldn't control in order to cover up the candidate's own responsibility
- Making unrealistic promises
- Evasiveness, such as avoiding answering questions about issues, giving ambiguous responses, or mentioning the benefits of a solution without giving specifics about how to carry out the solution

Beyond that list, look for evidence that candidates are staging public appearances to get attention from the press, such as rallies filled with patriotic paraphernalia and supporters clad in campaign shirts and buttons. Are candidates using these appearances to shout about what's wrong in the community or attack an opponent without offering their own specific ideas to solve problems? Also, keep an eye on campaign ads (especially on television or online) in which candidates viciously attack an opponent or appeal to people's patriotism and emotions instead of discussing their own qualifications and ideas. By identifying these manipulative campaign techniques, you can identify whether candidates are blowing smoke or if they're for real.

Take a hard look at their campaign activities using this advice from the LWV: "Do they give speeches to different groups—even those groups that may disagree with the candidates' views on issues? Do they accept invitations to debate? Do the campaigns emphasize media events, where the candidates can be seen but not heard?" (An example of a "seen but not heard" event is a candidate cutting a ribbon to open a new bridge rather than talking about real transportation issues facing the community. This type of appearance gives the impression of leadership and community involvement but it doesn't actually require candidates to prove they can address key issues.)

FIND OUT WHAT OTHERS THINK

Find out what other people in your community think of the candidates running in upcoming elections. Ask family members and community members (such as business owners or local volunteers) whom they support and why. Get a list of candidates' endorsements from interest groups or organizations. Learn what those groups represent and consider why they endorsed the candidate—is it because they believe the candidate will do good work to address community problems or because they hope the candidate will represent their interests once elected?

Find out who's donated to candidates' campaigns (a good source for this is the website www .opensecrets.org). How will these donations affect how candidates behave as elected officials? Will they

Figuring out whether a candidate deserves your support can be hard. To get perspective, ask people in your life and in the community what they think about the candidates.

feel compelled to, for instance, recommend a certain company for a government contract because someone from that company donated to their campaign?

What others think about a candidate can help you put your own thoughts and opinions into perspective. However, don't let their opinions undermine your own. You've done your research and thought about the candidates in terms of the things you care about. Use your instincts and your evidence as launchpads into political and community involvement.

 CHAPTER FOUR

IT'S YOUR TURN

However far away a problem like gun violence or climate change may seem from your personal experience, the causes of most problems are likely present in your community. For example, you may know people who struggle with emotional or developmental issues that, if untreated, may lead them to commit violence. Perhaps someone in your life has behaved in a way that you found concerning or offensive. Maybe your town doesn't recycle or make an effort to educate the public about environmental conservation. Perhaps the local animal shelter euthanizes far more animals than it gets adopted. All these scenarios present a chance for you to become involved in solving problems in your community.

Gareth Morgans has this advice:

Find something that you're passionate about and begin researching the issue. Find legitimate research to back up your passion and start researching who, within your community, is

What problems in your community do you care about? You don't have to be old enough to vote to do something about them. You can start making a difference now.

passionate about the same issue and how they are advocating for it. Are they working with their city council member or county commissioner? Maybe it's a state or federal issue and they're working with their state senator or member of Congress. Every voice counts during a discussion, and making sure your voice is heard is vital to both democracy and creating long-term, effective policy change.

WORKING WITHIN YOUR COMMUNITY

Overcoming the limitations of elected offices, confusion over how different levels of government work, and the pitfalls of party politics depends a great deal on people setting aside differences to work toward solutions. In her book *Smart Communities: How Citizens and Local Leaders Can Use Strategic Thinking to Build a Brighter Future*, Suzanne W. Morse says, "Democracy becomes real for people when they move beyond the political candidate or campaign they support and decide what kind of community they want."

Politics has become adversarial, with status quo leadership losing sight of what's best for everyone. This is where community comes in. As evidenced by Barack Obama's early days in Chicago, solutions don't have to come from the government alone. Communities and the people in them can make change happen, and, in the process, develop leaders and potential elected officials who understand everyday challenges. As Morse writes, "Communities need leaders who come through the ranks and from the rank and file … Leadership occurs when individuals step up to the plate on important issues and when they are prepared to take on the difficult work."

START LOCALLY

The students responsible for March for Our Lives don't just hold public rallies and chant about putting an end to gun violence. They have identified problems (gun violence and lax regulations regarding purchasing firearms), researched the specific issues underlying those problems, and continued to lobby the state and federal governments to address those issues. March for Our Lives may have grown into a national organization by identifying school shootings and gun violence as national issues, but it started as a response to a local issue: the school shooting in Parkland, Florida.

"All politics is local," says Morgan. He advises students to find neighborhood civic clubs, where they can get involved on a grassroots level and discuss

Young people, like those who started March for Our Lives, can identify, research, and brainstorm solutions to community problems. Elected officials should listen to what they have to say.

concerns with neighbors, community members, and civic club leaders. Those leaders often have direct contact with elected officials. Involvement in a local civic organization could provide you with a path directly to an elected representative who could do something about an issue you care about.

SPEAK UP

It's important for local government bodies, like city councils and school boards, to know the people they serve. The concerns and desires of the people in your community should dictate what those local governments do. Young people can get involved by visiting city hall to meet the mayor and city council members. They can sit in on a school board meeting. The town's and school district's websites should have information about the people elected to sit on these governing bodies as well as the agendas for upcoming meetings. These agendas can give you valuable information about what issues are up for a vote at upcoming meetings.

Your local representatives may be discussing or voting on an issue you care about at a future meeting. If not, you can attend their meetings and write them letters to voice your opinions and ask them to do something about an issue you care about. To make your arguments strong, pin down a community problem you care about (like the animals at the local shelter or your curriculum at school) and gather evidence about the issue. (For example, find out how many animals currently need adoption or compare your school's curriculum to that of other school districts.) Document the opinions of other people who share your concerns. Develop your opinion about what should change based on the evidence and what others think. Visualize the solution and use your documentation to back that solution up when you speak at a local government meeting or write a letter to your local elected officials.

A lot of communities have groups of people who are already active in trying to solve problems. Through the local animal shelter, for example, you may be able to find information about nonprofit groups dedicated to helping animals find homes. Ask someone at city hall about local groups that work to help the homeless, protect the environment, or work on other causes

By identifying problems in your community, you can likely find existing organizations that are addressing those problems. These organizations may appreciate your help.

you want to champion. These groups usually need all the help they can get from volunteers who can provide hands-on assistance, get the word out, help gather supplies, and add their voices to the call for change. The parent-teacher association might already be fighting for curriculum changes; these groups usually welcome input from students. Through your participation with existing groups that care about what you care about, your call to action can be even louder, increasing the chance that you'll be heard by elected officials—and get the attention of candidates looking for key issues to define their campaigns.

CAMPAIGNS IN YOUR COMMUNITY

In May 2017, eighteen-year-old Mikael "Mike" Floyd, a high school student in the Houston suburb of Pearland, Texas, defeated a two-term incumbent candidate in his school district's Board of Trustees election by winning 54 percent of the vote. In addition to his young age, Floyd faced other challenges, such as his opponent receiving high-profile endorsements and having actual experience on the Board of Trustees. "We were the underdog in every way imaginable," Floyd told the local CBS station, KHOU. Despite these challenges, Floyd became one of the youngest elected officials in the country. "Floyd attributed his election success to having firsthand experience as a student in the district (he was a senior at the time of his election), campaigning on the issues affecting families in the school district, a growing desire for anti-establishment candidates, and the

IT TAKES A VILLAGE

Former secretary of state and presidential nominee Hillary Clinton once wrote a book called *It Takes a Village*. In it, she put forward the view that raising children is a societal responsibility, and that many institutions—like family, extended family, neighbors, schools, faith communities, medical professionals, and social and governmental groups—are all responsible for ensuring that children get the attention and care they need to be successful and happy.

Every community, regardless of size, location, or demographics, has people who need help. In some communities, these people get the help they need. In others, there may be underlying problems preventing people in need from getting the help they need. These problems may include insufficient funding for schools, too few professionals available or willing to intervene in a troubled person's life, and too few proactive community members willing to step up to help someone who is alone and in trouble.

While Clinton's "it takes a village" philosophy was controversial—critics said individuals should be responsible for their own behavior rather than communities stepping in to help raise children—most people can probably agree that it's better to address community problems before they result in a tragedy. Identifying those problems, studying them, and actively addressing them are all actions young people can take to make their own communities better. What's more, young people can help governmental bodies, like school boards, city councils, state legislatures, and even Congress, better understand the problems their communities face.

desire for systemic change," Morgans, Houston-based political consultant, said.

Not every young person who wants to help make change happen has to run for local office, as Floyd did. You can start close to home with involvement in

![Many political campaigns rely on young people to get involved in all kinds of ways. Use your strengths and interests to find a candidate you'd like to help get elected.]

Many political campaigns rely on young people to get involved in all kinds of ways. Use your strengths and interests to find a candidate you'd like to help get elected.

civic clubs, as Morgans suggests, but you can also get involved by working with political campaigns. That's how Angel Rivera, the former Indianapolis City-County councilor, got his start. "There are many opportunities at the local level, including nonprofits and appointed boards, that can introduce a young person to public service," Rivera said. "I began by getting involved in campaigns and later in public boards. With effort, you can quickly become a change agent in your own community."

JOIN A CAMPAIGN

Campaigns are a great way to tackle an issue you care about while also helping a candidate who shares your concerns and vision for the future. Morgans said:

> Find an issue you're passionate about and find a candidate that supports that issue or has advocated for that issue in the past. Get involved with a candidate's campaign. Political campaigns are always looking for student organizers, volunteers, and Get Out the Vote (GOTV) squads. Find a candidate that you feel best shares your principles and contact their campaign. Ask to speak to a field organizer and explain why you're supporting the candidate and what skills you have that you feel would benefit the campaign.

If your research on candidates running for local, state, or federal office shows that none of those candidates is speaking about an issue you care about, contact the candidates' campaigns and ask them to consider adding your issue to the list of issues they're running on. Candidates may need your help identifying a problem in the community. Use your passion and research to get them to care about it, too.

RAISE YOUR VOICE

Whether through your school's student government, your town council or school board, your state and federal elected officials, or candidates' campaigns, you

Find a way to act on the things you care about. Participate in the political process on some level, whether it's at your school or in the broader community.

have many opportunities to make your voice heard. Don't pass up this chance. Young people can make an immense difference in the lives of many people. Public officials and candidates should take community problems seriously and work toward solving them, and young people can assist in that effort. It just takes a willingness to learn about community problems and the courage to bring those problems to the attention of public officials and candidates running for office. Even if you are not old enough to vote, that doesn't mean you don't have a voice. Speak up and make someone listen!

GLOSSARY

advocacy Support of a particular cause, policy, or group of people.

campaign To work toward the goal of getting elected to a public office.

candidate A person who runs for public office.

community A group of people who live in the same area or who have certain traits or characteristics in common.

community organizing Coordinating the efforts of local residents to further their community's interests.

Congress The two groups of elected officials—the House of Representatives and the Senate—that represent voters in national government.

election A process in which a group of people vote.

electorate The people who are entitled to vote in an election.

legislation Considering and making laws as part of a governing body.

legislature The legislative body of a country or state.

midterm election An election in which voters can elect representatives and other officeholders (such as state representatives or members of a local council) in the middle of the executive officer's term.

nonpartisan Not biased toward any particular political party, cause, or person.

party line A political party or group's official opinion, policy, or agenda.

platform The stated policy or policies of a political party, group, or candidate.

policy A course of action or principle proposed by or adopted by a government, party, or individual.

political party A group of people who work together because they share similar ideas.

representative A person chosen or elected to speak and act on behalf of others.

republic A country or state in which the power is held by the people and their elected representatives and which has an elected or nominated president.

term limits Restrictions on the number of times an elected representative can run for and hold a particular public office.

voter A person who has the right to cast a vote in an election.

voting base A group of voters who typically always support a single party's candidates for elected office.

Canadian Alliance of Student Associations (CASA)
130 Slater Street, Suite 410
Ottawa, ON, K1P 6E2
Canada
Website: http://www.casa-acae.com
Facebook, Instagram, and Twitter: @CASAACAE
CASA is a nonpartisan nonprofit student organization
composed of multiple student associations from
across Canada. The organization advocates for
students, and Canada's leaders consult with CASA
on decisions affecting the education system.

Inspire Democracy
30 Victoria Street
Gatineau, QC K1A 0M6
Canada
(800) 463-6868
Website: http://www.inspirerlademocratie
-inspiredemocracy.ca
Facebook: @ElectionsCanE
Twitter: @ElectionsCan_E
Inspire Democracy, an initiative of Elections Canada,
aims to encourage youth civic engagement. The
organization provides information on everything
from voter turnout and voter registration data to
civic participation and how political parties engage
with youth.

Millennial Action Project (MAP)
1875 Connecticut Avenue NW, 10th Floor
Washington, DC 20009

(202) 480-2051
Website: http://www.millennialaction.org
Facebook: @MillennialActionProject
Twitter: @MActionProject
MAP is the largest nonpartisan organization of
    millennial policymakers in the United States. The
    organization works to overcome partisanship
    through future-focused challenges and
    democracy reforms.

National Democratic Institute (NDI)
455 Massachusetts Avenue NW, 8th Floor
Washington, DC 20001
(202) 728-5500
Website: http://www.ndi.org
Facebook: @National.Democratic.Institute
Instagram: @ndidemocracy
Twitter: @NDI
NDI is a nonprofit nonpartisan organization that
    supports democratic institutions and practices
    all over the world. NDI promotes openness and
    accountability in government by building political
    and civic organizations, safeguarding elections, and
    promoting citizen participation.

Reboot Democracy
Website: http://www.rebootdem.com
Facebook, Instagram, and Twitter: @RebootDem
This nonprofit creates a comprehensive ecosystem
    of support for early-stage innovators who are
    building technology to strengthen democracy. The
    organization helps other innovative groups and

individuals, especially women and minorities, to connect and collaborate.

She Should Run
80 M Street SE, Floor 1
Washington, DC 20003
(202) 796-8396
Website: http://www.sheshouldrun.org
Facebook, Instagram, and Twitter: @sheshouldrun
She Should Run provides community, resources, and
   growth opportunities for women who are interested
   in running for public office.

Youth Service America (YSA)
1050 Connecticut Avenue NW, Room 65525
Washington, DC 20035
(202) 296-2992
Website: http://www.ysa.org or http://leadasap.ysa.org
Facebook: @youthserviceamerica
Twitter: @youthservice
YSA supports a global culture of engaged children and
   youth committed to a lifetime of meaningful service,
   learning, and leadership. The YSA websites feature
   the stories of young people who make a difference
   in their communities, encouraging newcomers to
   make a difference on their own.

FOR FURTHER READING

Cunningham, Kevin. *How Political Campaigns and Elections Work*. Minneapolis, MN: Core Library, 2015.

Fleischer, Jeff. *Votes of Confidence: A Young Person's Guide to American Elections*. San Francisco, CA: Zest Books, 2016.

Gunderson, Jessica. *Understanding Your Role in Elections*. North Mankato, MN: Capstone Press, 2018.

Harper, Leslie. *How to Contact an Elected Official*. New York, NY: Rosen Publishing, 2015.

Houser, Grace. *Understanding US Elections and the Electoral College*. New York, NY: Rosen Publishing, 2018.

Jacobs, Natalie, and Thomas A. Jacobs. *Every Vote Matters: The Power of Your Voice, From Student Elections to the Supreme Court*. Minneapolis, MN: Free Spirit Publishing, 2016.

Klepeis, Alicia Z. *Understanding the Electoral College*. New York, NY: Rosen Publishing, 2018.

Loria, Laura. *What Is the Constitution?* New York, NY: Rosen Publishing, 2016.

Machajewski, Sarah. *What Are State and Local Governments*? New York, NY: Rosen Publishing, 2016.

Martin, Bobi. *What Are Elections?* New York, NY: Rosen Publishing, 2016.

Small, Cathleen. *Elections and Voting*. New York, NY: Lucent Press, 2019.

Weiss, Nancy E. *Asking Questions About Political Campaigns*. Ann Arbor, MI: Cherry Lake Publishing, 2016.

BIBLIOGRAPHY

Aguilar, Julián. "Beto O'Rourke and Other Democrats Urge Public to Keep Tornillo Migrant Facility in Spotlight." *Texas Tribune*, December 15, 2018. https://www.texastribune.org/2018/12/15/beto -orourke-democrats-tornillo.

Aguilar, Julián, and Juan Luis García Hernández. "Beto O'Rourke, Veronica Escobar lead Father's Day March on Tent City Housing Separated Immigrant Children." *Texas Tribune*, June 17, 2018.https://www .texastribune.org/2018/06/17/texas-beto-orourke -tent-city-tornillo-immigration.

Berkowitz, Bill. "Section 5. Analyzing Community Problems." Community Tool Box, Center for Community Health and Development at the University of Kansas. Retrieved January 29, 2019. https://ctb.ku.edu/en/table-of-contents/assessment /assessing-community-needs-and-resources /analyzing-community-problems/main.

Berman, Mark, et al. "Florida Shooting Suspect Nikolas Cruz: Guns, Depression and a Life in Trouble." *Washington Post*, February 15, 2018. https://www .washingtonpost.com/news/morning-mix /wp/2018/02/15/florida-shooting-suspect-nikolas -cruz-guns-depression-and-a-life-in-free-fall/?utm _term=.e71ccb1cd9dd.

Bernstein, Jackie. "4 Problems in Your Community That Need Your Attention & How You Can Help." Bustle, November 3, 2015. https://www.bustle.com /articles/118926-4-problems-in-your-community-that -need-your-attention-how-you-can-help.

Bump, Philip. "Eighteen Years of Gun Violence in US Schools, Mapped." *Washington Post*, February 14, 2018. https://www.washingtonpost.com/news/politics /wp/2018/02/14/eighteen-years-of-gun-violence -in-u-s-schools-mapped/?noredirect=on&utm _term=.7d41f25864ee.

Bump, Philip. "4.4 million 2012 Obama Voters Stayed Home in 2016 — More Than a Third of Them Black." *Washington Post*, March 12, 2018. https://www .washingtonpost.com/news/politics /wp/2018/03/12/4-4-million-2012-obama-voters -stayed-home-in-2016-more-than-a-third-of-them black/?noredirect=on&utm_term=.8f57e8f6e2d3.

Chuck, Elizabeth, Alex Johnson, and Corky Siemaszko. "17 Killed in Mass Shooting at High School in Parkland, Florida." NBC News, February 14, 2018. https://www.nbcnews.com/news/us-news /police-respond-shooting-parkland-florida-high -school-n848101.

Hogg, David (@davidhogg111). "Dear Politicians, Don't call us asking for endorsements. The only thing we endorse is common sense policies. Don't call us asking for political donations. If you need money from special interest groups then you shouldn't be running. Sincerely, March For Our Lives." Twitter, July 12, 2018. https://twitter.com/davidhogg111 /status/1017528364507131904.

Kovaleski, Serge. "Obama's Organizing Years, Guiding Others and Finding Himself." *New York Times*, July 7, 2008. http://www.nytimes.com/2008/07/07/us /politics/07community.html.

League of Women Voters. "How to Judge a Candidate." August 19, 2008. https://www.lwv.org/educating -voters/how-judge-candidate.

Marcotte, Amanda. "Hillary Clinton Defies Right-Wing Critics, Endorses Universal Pre-K." Slate, June 18, 2015. https://slate.com/human-interest/2015/06 /conservatives-hate-it-takes-a-village-hillary-clinton -embraces-it-by-endorsing-universal-pre-k.html.

Mazzei, Patricia. "Parkland Shooting Suspect Lost Special-Needs Help at School When He Needed It Most." *New York Times*, April 4, 2018. https://www .nytimes.com/2018/08/04/us/parkland-florida -nikolas-cruz.html.

McLaughlin, Eliot C., and Madison Park. "School Shooter's Past Includes Buying Guns, Cutting, Slurs and Mental Illness." CNN, February 20, 2018. http:// www.cnn.com/2018/02/19/us/florida-school-shooting /index.html.

Meyer, Cheryl Diaz, Becky Harlan, and Eric Lee. "Students Make Their Stand at DC's 'March For Our Lives.'" National Public Radio, March 25, 2018. https://www.npr.org/2018/03/25/596760836/photos -students-make-their-stand-at-d-c-s-march-for-our -lives.

Morgans, Gareth (political consultant). In discussion with the author, Houston, Texas, March 6, 2019.

Morse, Suzanne W. *Smart Communities: How Citizens and Local Leaders Can Use Strategic Thinking to Build a Brighter Future*. San Francisco, CA: Jossey -Bass, 2014.

National Democratic Institute. "Campaign Skills Trainer's Guide: Identifying Issues and Developing Policy Positions." Retrieved January 25, 2019. https://www.ndi.org.

Rivera, Angel (former Indianapolis City-County Councillor). In discussion with the author, Irving, Texas, February 6, 2019.

Robillard, Kevin. "Study: Youth Vote Was Decisive." Politico, November 7, 2012. https://www.politico .com/story/2012/11/study-youth-vote-was -decisive-083510.

Schwartzman, Edward. *Political Campaign Craftsmanship: A Professional's Guide to Campaigning for Public Office.* New York, NY: Routledge, 2017.

Smith, Brandi. "Pearland Student, 18, Beats Incumbent for School Board Seat." KHOU, May 7, 2017. https:// www.khou.com/article/news/local/pearland -student-18-beats-incumbent-for-school-board -seat/285-437624238.

INDEX

ABOUT THE AUTHOR

Angie Timmons is a writer and communications consultant who has worked on two US congressional campaigns and one state campaign leading up to the 2018 midterm elections. She cochairs the communications committee of a local women's political group and is active in other political and activist organizations. She has written multiple books for Rosen Publishing, including histories of World War II, the Cold War, the Nanjing Massacre, and racism, with a heavy emphasis on the politics behind those subjects. She lives with her husband and their three cats in the Dallas area.

PHOTO CREDITS

Cover Marc Romanelli/Getty Images; pp. 4–5 (background graphics) weerawan/iStock/Getty Images; p. 5 Paul Morigi/Getty Images; p. 8 Joseph Sohm/Shutterstock.com; p. 9 William Thomas Cain/Getty Images; p. 11 Simone Hogan/Shutterstock.com; p. 14 Irina Boriskina/Shutterstock.com; pp. 15, 24, 26 Bloomberg/Getty Images; p. 19 Spencer Platt/Getty Images; p. 21 Paul Ratje/AFP/Getty Images; p. 29 Don Emmert/AFP/Getty Images; pp. 31, 45 Jeffrey Greenberg/UIG/Getty Images; p. 33 Andrew Lichtenstein/Corbis News/Getty Images; p. 35 NurPhoto/Getty Images; p. 39 gawrav/E+/Getty Images; p. 41 Dragon Images/Shutterstock.com; p. 43 Brendan Smialowski/AFP/Getty Images; p. 48 Barbara Davidson/Getty Images; p. 50 Jupiter Images/Photos.com/Getty Images; additional graphic elements moodboard - Mike Watson Images/Brand X Pictures/Getty Images (chapter opener backgrounds), Maksim M/Shutterstock.com (fists).

Design and Layout: Michael Moy; Editor: Rachel Aimee; Photo Researcher: Nicole DiMella

Shirley Barber's

FAIRY STORIES
and CD

Table of Contents

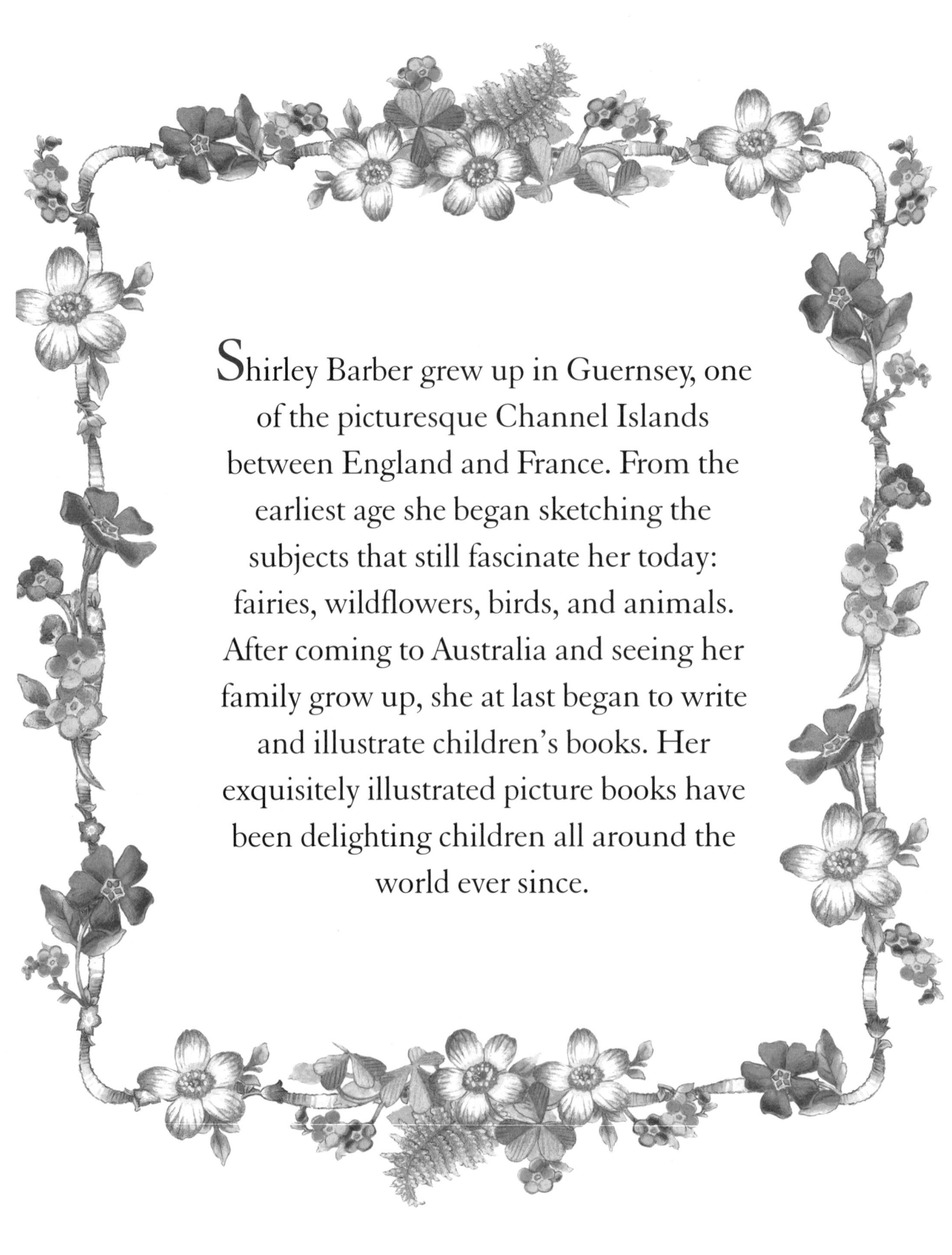

Shirley Barber grew up in Guernsey, one of the picturesque Channel Islands between England and France. From the earliest age she began sketching the subjects that still fascinate her today: fairies, wildflowers, birds, and animals. After coming to Australia and seeing her family grow up, she at last began to write and illustrate children's books. Her exquisitely illustrated picture books have been delighting children all around the world ever since.

A Visit to
FAIRYLAND

Laura said there were fairies at the bottom of the garden. She said that in the old willow tree there was a green door and when the fairies opened it you could see right into Fairyland.

"Yes, dear," said her mother, who was busy cooking. "Now, why don't you take your little brother into the garden? You can show him the fairies and the door to Fairyland."

Laura could tell that her mother thought she was just pretending and she felt rather hurt. Still, she took Daniel's hand and led him into the garden and down towards the willow tree.

"Ssh, Danny," she whispered. "If we are very quiet the fairies might open their green door and come out to talk to us."

Sure enough, after a few minutes the green door opened... and out came the fairies.

"Would you like to come through this little doorway and see Fairyland?" asked the fairies.

"Oh, yes!" exclaimed Laura excitedly. Then she and Daniel crawled through the doorway and found themselves in Fairyland.

Before them was a toadstool town where pixies and other fairy folk were busy shopping and chatting, just like people. Daniel trotted off chuckling to explore the narrow twisting streets.

"Don't go too far, you might get lost," warned his sister. "Stay close so I can keep an eye on you!"

To Daniel the toadstool houses were just like a toy village and he wanted to play with the pixies. Laura watched him running about for a while, then she noticed further away a garden full of big flowers.

"Come along, Danny," she coaxed. "Let's go and look at those beautiful flowers."

The flowers were so large that Daniel soon forgot the toadstool houses and ran to look at them. Inside each flower a fairy baby was curled up as if in its cradle.

"This is where our babies live till they are old enough to fly," a fairy nurse told the children.

The flower nursery was bathed in warm golden light and soon the children were glad to go into some nearby woods where it was cool and shady. A fern-fringed path led them to a lily pool where fairies were bathing and playing near a crystal spring. Laura and Daniel drank springwater from leaf-cups, and paddled in the shallows. Soon they felt cool enough to explore further.

They followed the path through the woods and before long they heard sweet music: pipes, bells and a tinkling harp. Then, in a clearing edged with flowers, they came upon a group of elfin musicians. Rabbits, mice, and frogs all had their parts to play and several fairies were dancing to music.

"There is a ball tonight," the fairies explained to the children, "so we are practicing our steps!"

The children wandered on and soon they came to the edge of the woods. There, between twisted tree roots, large caves had formed in a sandy bank. Inside each cave was a kitchen in which elfin cooks were preparing a marvelous feast.

"All these lovely dishes will be served at the ball tonight," the fairies told the children. "The food is cooked here, then taken to the fairy castle in butterfly carriages."

Of course the children felt hungry seeing such lovely food, so the kindly elves invited them to sit down and eat whatever they liked.

While they tried all kinds of dainty and colorful cakes and biscuits, Laura talked to the fairies and elves about life in Fairyland.

"Do you ever have to do any work?" she asked.

"Oh, yes," one silver-haired fairy replied. "My work is to go out and put frost crystals everywhere."

"Why do you do that?" Laura asked, puzzled.

"Well, when the world has been dull and gloomy and you wake to a day where every twig and grass blade sparkles, it's suddenly a beautiful surprise, isn't it?"

"Oh, yes it is," cried Laura. "Thank you, Silver Fairy, for all your lovely frosty mornings!"

"I too have my work in the world," said an elf, smiling at Laura and Daniel. "With my baskets of toadstools I fly around at first light and I plant bright red ones where I think they will look just right."

"Yes, we've seen them, haven't we, Daniel?" cried Laura excitedly. "You left some spotted ones under the pine trees just outside our garden."

"Now, what would you like to
see next?" the fairies asked the children.

Laura looked at Daniel. "We ought to be going home," she
said regretfully. "Our Aunt Kathy is coming to lunch at
our house, and it will be ready soon."

But Daniel wasn't ready to go home, and Laura was afraid
he would make a fuss, so she decided they could stay in
Fairyland for just a little while longer.

"Can we see where you make all your pretty sparkling
dresses?" she asked the fairies.

So the fairies showed the children the little silk spinners
who spend all their time making gossamer-fine
shawls, cloaks and dresses, all delicately
sewn with diamond droplets.

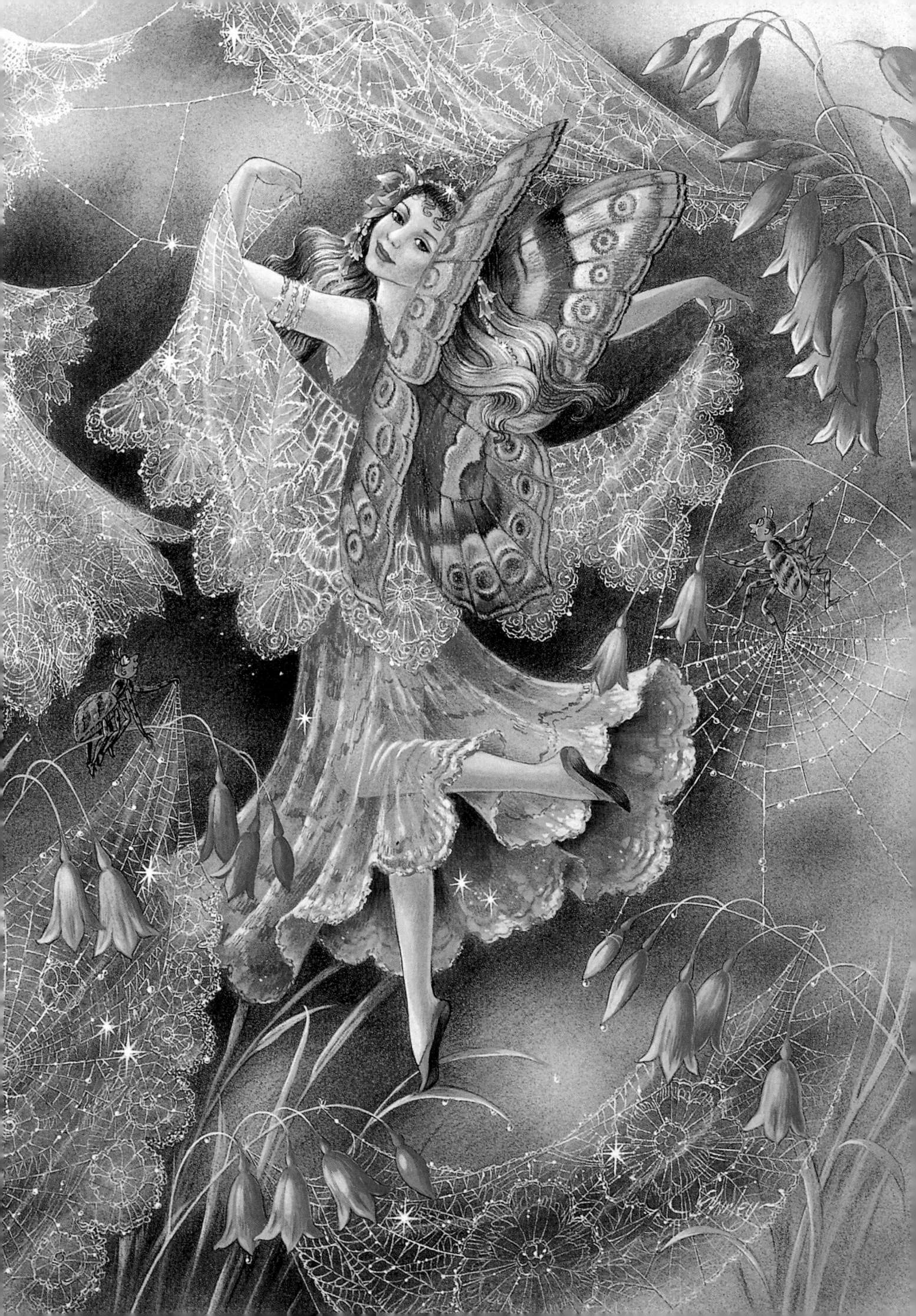

"Please show us one last thing before we go home," said Laura. "We'd love to see the fairy castle where you live and where the ball will be held tonight."

So the fairies put Laura and Daniel into a butterfly carriage which floated over the sea to a bay of islands, where a glittering fairy castle stood upon a rocky pinnacle.

While they were circling the castle, Daniel fell asleep in the butterfly carriage. It flew over the forest, the big flowers, and the toadstool town before landing at last near the old willow tree.

Laura woke up Daniel, and while he was
still too sleepy to protest she helped him
crawl back through the little doorway.

"Goodbye, Laura and Daniel," called the fairies.
"Be good and kind, and you will see us again
soon."

Then the little green door shut and seemed to
fade away.

"Come along, Danny," said Laura. "Let's go and
have lunch, and we'll tell Mommy all about
our visit to Fairyland."

The children found their mother just laying the table for lunch. Their Aunt Kathy had arrived, and she hugged the children and gave each of them a drawing book and a packet of coloring pencils.

"Danny's very good at drawing," Laura told her. "He can draw a box, a ball, and a happy face. Danny, draw something for Aunt Kathy."

So Daniel drew a picture. But everyone was very surprised when he didn't draw a box or a ball or a happy face - he drew a fairy instead!

FAIRY BOOK
An Anthology of Verse

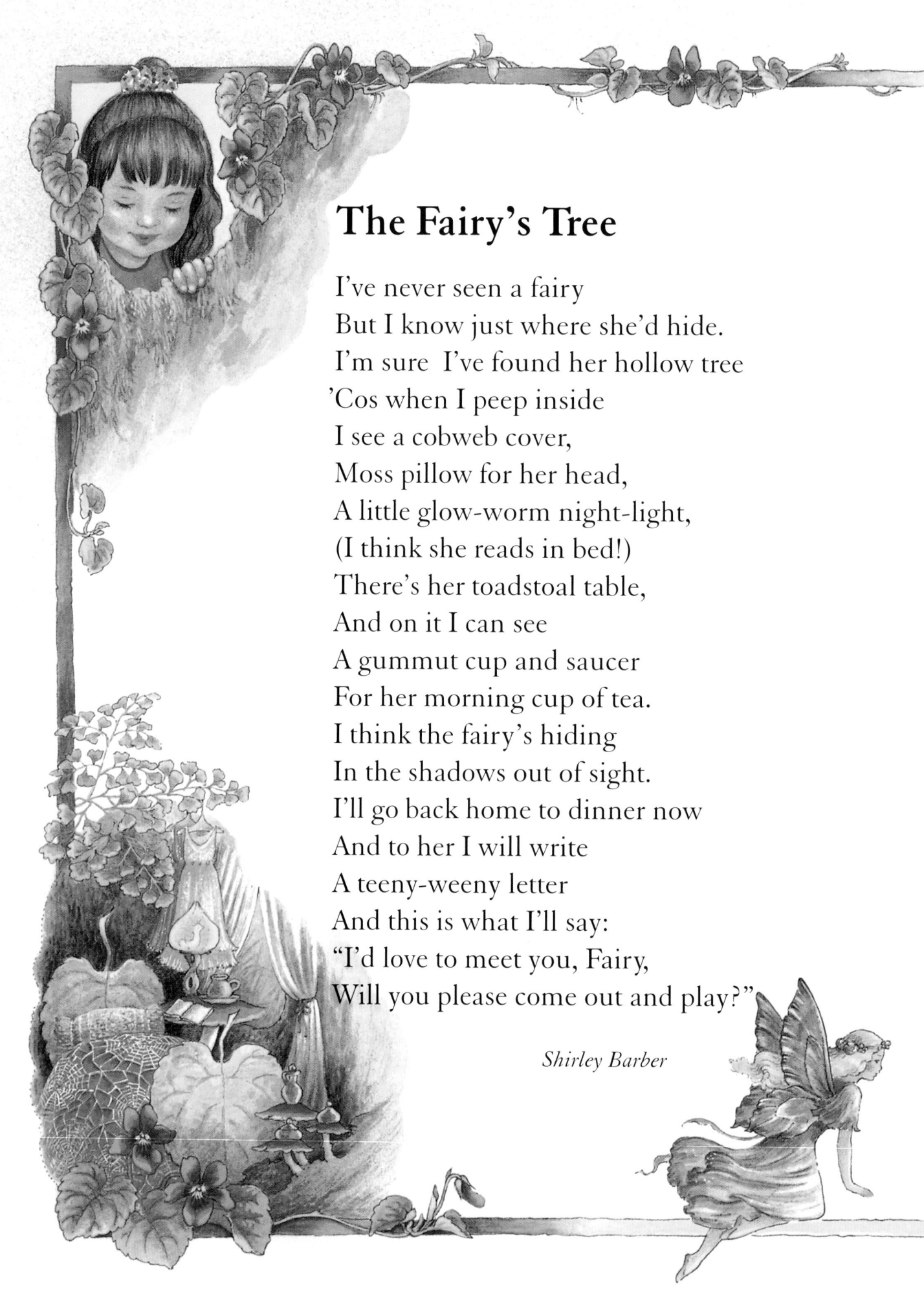

The Fairy's Tree

I've never seen a fairy
But I know just where she'd hide.
I'm sure I've found her hollow tree
'Cos when I peep inside
I see a cobweb cover,
Moss pillow for her head,
A little glow-worm night-light,
(I think she reads in bed!)
There's her toadstoal table,
And on it I can see
A gummut cup and saucer
For her morning cup of tea.
I think the fairy's hiding
In the shadows out of sight.
I'll go back home to dinner now
And to her I will write
A teeny-weeny letter
And this is what I'll say:
"I'd love to meet you, Fairy,
Will you please come out and play?"

Shirley Barber

Toadstools

It's not a bit windy,
It's not a bit wet,
The sky is as sunny
As summer, and yet
Little umbrellas are
Everywhere spread,
Pink ones, and brown ones,
And orange, and red.

I can't see the folks
Who are hidden below;
I've peeped, and I've peeped
Round the edges but no!
They hold their umbrellas
So tight and so close
That nothing shows under,
Not even a nose!

Elizabeth Fleming

Bedtime Story

Tell me my favorite story
While I am snuggling down,
About the beautiful fairy
Who wears a sparkling gown.

Tell me about her silken hair,
Her rainbow-colored wings,
Tell of her bag of magic stars,
Sing me the song she sings.

Tell me she flies through the forest dark
And after a while she hears
A poor little bunny crying,
So, gently she dries his tears.

She carries him home to his burrow
So he's just in time for tea.
(His mother was looking out for him
Just as you look for me!)

For an hour or so she lingers.
She sings the bunny to sleep,
Then leaves behind on his pillow
A magical star to keep.

I'll help you remember the wording.
It has to be told just right.
And then you can tell me it
all again
Tomorrow – and every night!

Shirley Barber

The Flowers

All the names I know from nurse:
Gardener's Garters, Shepherd's Purse;
Bachelor's Buttons, Lady's Smock,
And the Lady Hollyhock.

Fairy places, fairy things,
Fairy woods where the wild bee wings,
Tiny trees for tiny dames –
These must all be fairy names!

Tiny woods below whose boughs
Shady fairies weave a house;
Tiny treetops, rose or thyme,
Where the braver fairies climb!

Fair are grown up people's trees,
But the fairest woods are these;
Where, if I were not so tall,
I should live for good and all.

Robert Louis Stevenson

The Miniature World

If I was very, very small
The jointed grasses would be tall,
And I would climb up them like trees
To wave to passing honey bees.
And then I think I'd like to try
To ride a big blue dragonfly –
Zigzag around the sky like mad
Then land it on a lily-pad.
When I was hungry I would eat
Sorrel, mint and meadow-sweet.
Maybe I'd leapfrog real frogs,
Or maybe dive off mossy logs
Into pools deep, cool, and dim,
And with the little tadpoles swim.
Of course, it would be very scary
Meeting spiders, black and hairy!
And those giant drops of dew –
I guess I'd have to dodge them too!
But it would be so nice to know
The hidden paths where Fairies go,
And oh! so good to spend my days
Exploring, secret forest ways...
And when I was too tired to roam
I'd hail a beetle and ride home!

Shirley Barber

The Fairies' Ball

Katie has a fine doll's house,
It stands against the wall;
Her grandma gave it to her and
It's elegant and tall.

Katie said, at midnight,
Or perhaps a little after,
She was woken by the tiny sounds
Of music and of laughter.

She sat up in her bed and thought
She really must be dreaming –
From every little doll's house window
Golden light was streaming.

She crept across to see what could
Be going on in there,
And saw it was a fairies' ball –
A very grand affair.

All night the fairies reveled, then
At dawn, away they flew.
Now Katie's just a little cross
At all there is to do.

She doesn't mind her doll's house used
By fairies and by elves,
But thinks that they should always
Clean up afterwards themselves!

Shirley Barber

The Rainbow Stairway

The lightning made us jump,
The thunder was much too loud,
The rain came down in a torrent,
But now, against the cloud,
The garden glows in the sunlight;
We stare at the golden hill. For look!
Through the sparkling raindrops,
Which gently shower still,
There's a rainbow stairway curving
Down from the sky's gray-blue,
So fairies can climb to their ballroom
Shall we run and climb it too?

Shirley Barber

The Fairy Swing

Down in the apple orchard
White petals fell like rain
Round little Mary Catherine
As she made a daisy-chain.

She used a lot of daisies,
She fashioned it with care –
Heard her mother calling her,
And left it hanging there.

When later she went back again
She heard a wee voice singing,
And in her daisy-chain she saw
A lovely fairy swinging.

Now, Mary Catherine always leaves
Her daisy-chains behind.
If fairies use them for their swings
She says she doesn't mind.

Shirley Barber

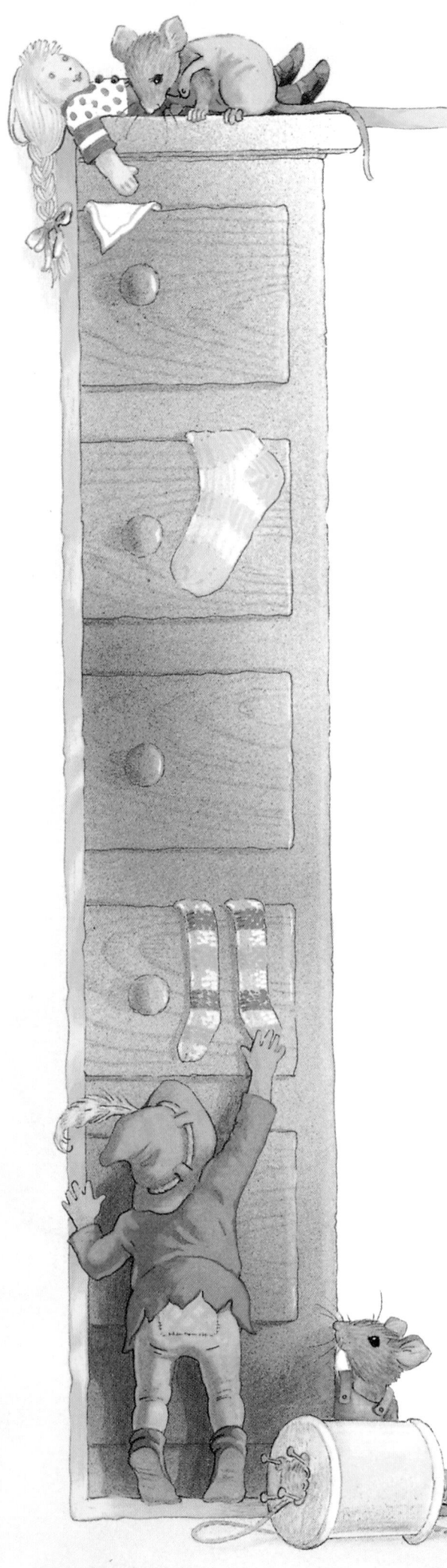

Elfin Friends

Uncle William knew an elf,
"A manikin," he said,
"In pointed hat and buckled shoes
And a suit of green and red."

Aunt Betty knew an elf
Of whom she grew quite fond.
They quarelled when he tried to fish
The goldfish from her pond.

My grandma said a little elf
She often used to see.
He'd visit her to chat and drink
A thimbleful of tea.

She knitted him a woolly cap
With flaps to warm his ears,
And he was very grateful –
They were friends for years and years.

They teach you really silly things
When first you go to school,
Like knitting useless woolly snakes
Right through a wooden spool.

But I had such a good idea –
In red and green and white
I've knitted socks for chilly elves,
(I hope they're not too bright!)

If I can stay awake tonight,
And if there is an elf,
And if he likes his socks, I'll have
An elfin friend myself.

Shirley Barber

The Little Elfman

I met a little elfman once,
Down where the lilies blow.
I asked him why he was so small.
And why he didn't grow.

He slightly frowned, and with his eye
He looked me through and through –
"I'm just as big for me," said he,
"As you are big for you!"

John Kendrick Bangs

The Tea Party

A robin brought the message –
She'll come at half-past three.
We'll sit where it is shady
Beneath the willow tree.
I'll make some tiny sandwiches,
Fill flower cups with dew.
A pollen cake I'll try to make
And daisy biscuits too.
I'll lay upon this toadstool
Rose petal plates for three.
The table must look pretty when
A Fairy comes to tea.

Shirley Barber

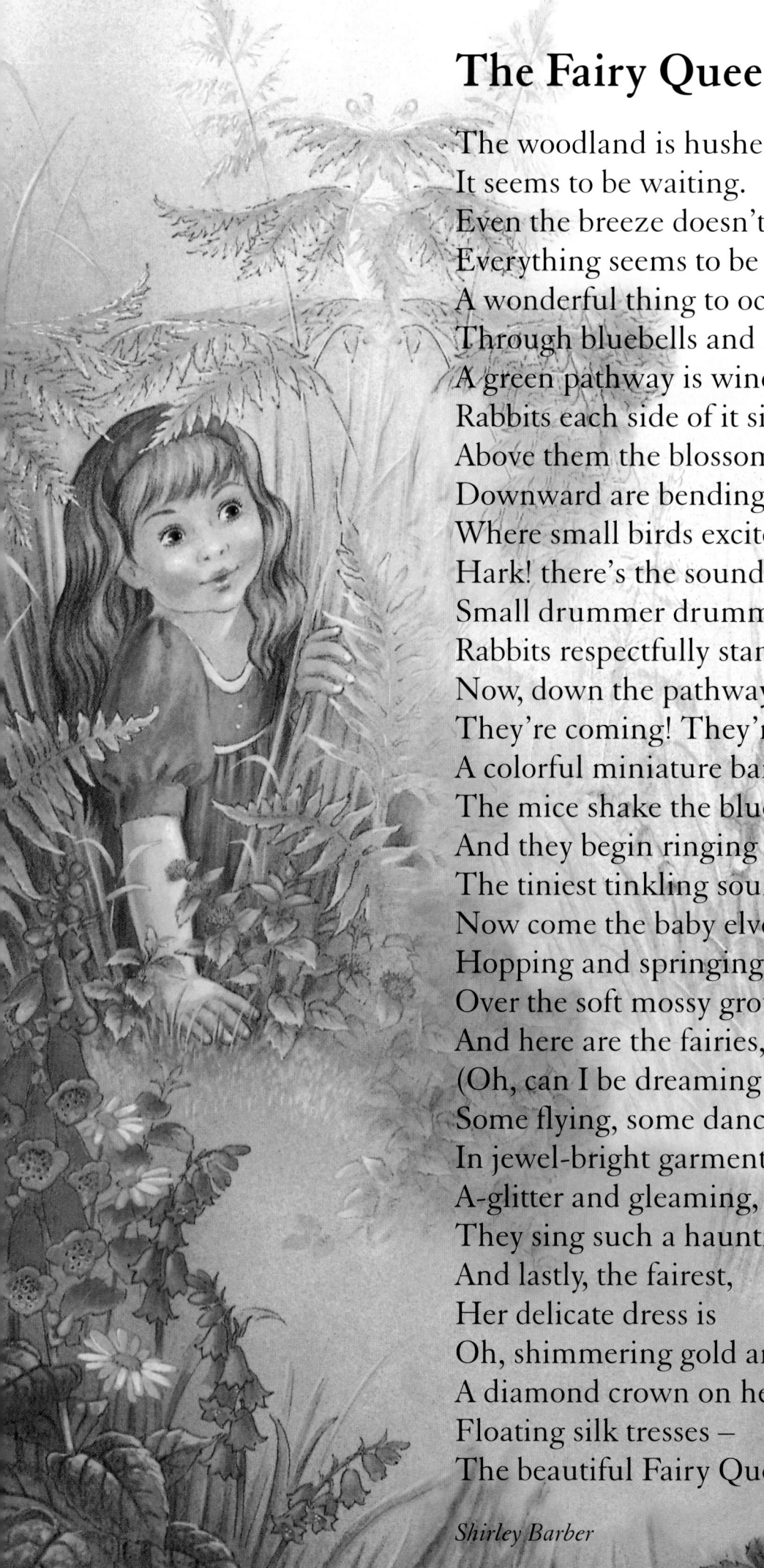

The Fairy Queen

The woodland is hushed –
It seems to be waiting.
Even the breeze doesn't stir.
Everything seems to be anticipating
A wonderful thing to occur.
Through bluebells and ferns
A green pathway is winding;
Rabbits each side of it sit.
Above them the blossom boughs
Downward are bending
Where small birds excitedly flit.
Hark! there's the sound of a
Small drummer drumming.
Rabbits respectfully stand.
Now, down the pathway
They're coming! They're coming!
A colorful miniature band!
The mice shake the bluebells
And they begin ringing –
The tiniest tinkling sound.
Now come the baby elves
Hopping and springing
Over the soft mossy ground.
And here are the fairies,
(Oh, can I be dreaming?) –
Some flying, some dancing along.
In jewel-bright garments
A-glitter and gleaming,
They sing such a haunting sweet song.
And lastly, the fairest,
Her delicate dress is
Oh, shimmering gold and pale green;
A diamond crown on her
Floating silk tresses –
The beautiful Fairy Queen!

Shirley Barber

Fairy Dresses

The other day I woke at dawn,
And tiptoed out onto the lawn,
Then I stared in such surprise
At the sight which met my eyes.
Everywhere I looked there were
Veils of jeweled gossamer.
Where the hollyhocks grow tall
Fairy shawls lay over all;
On the rose-arch, in each space,
Petticoats of finest lace.
On the lupins and the phlox
Hung the daintiest fairy frocks,
Diamond-sprinkled, shimmering,
And, in shadows glimmering,
Sequined cloaks for evening wear;
Twinkling strands for golden hair.
Someone, (hiding I suppose),
Must have fashioned all those clothes,
Hoped a fairy passing by
Would fly down her dress to buy.
But – whose fingers, small but strong
Had been so busy all night long?

Shirley Barber

Fairy-wear

A Cowslip flower will make a hat
  for any little elf;
With Pennywort umbrellas he
  can always shade himself.
Wild Arum makes both hood and cape
  if it should start to rain,
At night a Lamb's Ear leaf can be
  his furry counterpane.

In the hedge, Convolvulus
  has flowers light and airy;
Neatly pleated flaring dresses
  fit for any fairy.
A spangled wrap of lacy webs
  draped softly over all,
A crown of Hawthorn buds and she
  is ready for the ball.

Shirley Barber

Water Babies

Where do the Water Babies dwell –
Does anyone know, can anyone tell?
"Yes," said a mermaid sweet to me,
"They live beside the bright blue sea.

"Down on the sands they come and play,
They paddle in the sea all day;
With tiny dimpled naked feet,
I've seen them!" cried a mermaid sweet.

And she was right – I've seen them too,
Little white feet in the water blue;
Scampering merrily hand in hand,
All along the golden sand.

No wonder the sea laughs all day long.
And sings them such a happy song;
I've seen them there, so I know well,
That's where the Water Babies dwell.

Unknown

The Mermaid's Child

Down by the sea Louisa found
A mermaid's baby (so she said).
It lay within an ormer shell,
Curled up as if that was its bed.

She fed it sea-foam cake and when
It cried she gave its face a kiss.
She combed its curls, and cuddled it –
Oh! we got very tired of this!

She wouldn't swim or play with us
She stayed beside it all the day.
Thank goodness when the tide came in
The mermaids took their child away.

Shirley Barber

The Dream Fairy

A little fairy comes at night,
Her eyes are blue, her hair is brown,
With silver spots upon her wings,
And from the moon she flutters down.

She has a little silver wand,
And when a good child goes to bed
She waves her wand from right to left
And makes a circle round her head.

And then it dreams of pleasant things,
Of fountains filled with fairy fish,
And trees that bear delicious fruit,
And bow their branches at a wish;

Of arbors filled with dainty scents
From lovely flowers that never fade,
Bright 'flies that flitter in the sun,
And glow-worms shining in the shade;

And talking birds with gifted tongues
For singing songs and telling tales,
And pretty dwarfs to show the way
Through the fairy hills and fairy dales.

Thomas Hood

The Little Folk

In Spring, when the cherry-plum blossom
Lay soft as pink foam in the trees,
I saw them descend on the garden.
At first, sure, I thought it was bees!

Down where the petals were scattered,
Laughing and singing they came.
I watched from my window astonished –
The Little Folk playing a game.

They swung from the flower-laden branches.
They twisted and spun on the wing.
Their singing was sweeter than silver
As they sang and they danced in a ring.

Well! I never saw a sight like it –
The Little Folk all at their play.
Then Pussy ran out from the bushes,
And up they all flew – and away!

Shirley Barber

Midnight Fishing

The crescent moon is riding high
Like a silver ship in the midnight sky.
Those misty veils
Are silken sails
And we can go fishing, you and I.

We'll rock on waves of deepest blue.
We'll cast our nets like the sailors do.
Each shining fish
Is a tiny wish,
And we'll make sure to bring home a few.

We'll moor by a cloud in Scorpio.
You're much braver than I am, so
Lean out and grab
A spangled crab
While I drop my line in the depths below.

We're sailing home by dawn's pink light.
With a glittering crab and the wishes bright,
The silvery gleam
Of a fisherman's dream –
Oh! let's go fishing again tonight.

Shirley Barber

Twelve O'Clock — Fairy-time

Through the house give glimmering light
By the dead and drowsy fire;
Every elf and fairy sprite
Hop as light as bird from brier.

. . .

Now, until the break of day,
Through this house each fairy stray.

William Shakespeare

THE MERMAID PRINCESS

In a tropical ocean lay a small green island surrounded by sandy beaches and a coral reef. At high tide, when the sea covered the reef, it flowered like a magical garden - filled with brilliant fish, swaying plants and strange sea creatures. There was only one house on the island in it lived two children, Jon and Wendy, and their parents.

It was holiday time. Jon and Wendy's father spent all day in his boat fishing, and their mother was busy writing a book. Wendy was recovering from the flu, and was too weak to do anything. She just lay on a couch gazing out to sea, or down into the big coral pool not far from her window. Nothing seemed to interest her.

Jon spent his time wandering over the reef at low tide.
When he found something really unusual he would bring it
inside to show Wendy. All the while, he was being
watched by someone very small hidden amongst the coral.
It was Sandy the seashore pixie. Sandy lived in a
sandcastle decorated with bits of green and white
sea-smoothed glass.

Early each morning, Sandy pushed his little cart along the tide-line to see what had been washed up. He found bean pods and shells, which he used to keep things in, and sticks for his fire. But what he liked to find most were pieces of colored glass. He always hoped to find really colorful ones, of sparkling red or blue, but somehow he never did.

One morning, Sandy was amazed to find a beautiful mermaid sitting amidst the coral. She told Sandy that her name was Marina, and that she had been riding on her pet dolphin Silverfin when they were suddenly chased by a huge shark. The dolphin had tossed her ashore, so she would be safe, and then sped off. "But I cut my tail on the sharp coral," she told the pixie, "So now I can't swim home."

Sandy didn't know what to do. He knew that when the tide returned it would sweep the mermaid over the sharp coral and she would be hurt again. Just then Jon appeared on the reef. Sandy quickly hid. To the little pixie, Jon was as big as a giant.

"A real mermaid!" exclaimed Jon. "I've just got to show her to Wendy!" He carefully picked up Marina and carried her back to the coral pool near his sister's window.

Jon ran inside the house. "Wendy!" he called. "I've found a real-live mermaid. I've put her in your coral pool so you can see her through your window."

Wendy sat up and looked out at the pool. Sure enough, there was the mermaid. She was calmly tidying her golden hair. At last something *did* interest Wendy! "Isn't she beautiful!" she cried.

"Yes, but we must keep her a secret," said Jon, "or she might be taken away and put in an aquarium."

That night, when the moon had risen high in the sky, Wendy awoke with a start. She looked out of the window. Yes, the mermaid was still there - and she was talking to a tiny figure! Wendy got up rather shakily and tiptoed to wake Jon. Together they slipped out of the house and down to the coral pool.

At first the mermaid and pixie were too shy to answer Jon and Wendy's eager questions.

"Please talk to us," Wendy begged. "We only want to help you." So Sandy introduced himself and Marina to the children. Then Marina told them her story.

"Somehow we must tell Marina's people where she is so they can come and fetch her," said Jon when she had finished. "I could go," said Sandy. "I have a boat."

Sandy said he would anchor his boat at the edge of the reef and dive down to look for the mermaid's underwater city.

"But how will you breath under water?" asked Jon.

"Seashore pixies can breathe under water as well as on land," Sandy replied.

Marina said he would need a snack for the journey, and gave him some dainty kelp biscuits.

Sandy sailed out over the reef and anchored just beyond it. Then he bravely let himself sink down through the dark water till he landed on the sea-floor. With each surge of the sea he could hear a bell softly chiming. Faint lights glimmered in the distance. Sandy set off over the sand towards them, feeling sure they were coming from the underwater city.

He walked all night. When the sun rose, a soft radiance lit the underwater world, Sandy could now see huge shipwrecks on the sea-floor. Not far from them were open treasure chests which spilled jewels onto the sand. To Sandy the jewels looked like the prettiest bits of colored glass he had ever seen. He longed to pick some up and take them home, but he didn't because he felt sure they belonged to the mer-people.

At last he could see the underwater city in the distance. He was almost at the end of his journey.

Suddenly shoals of fish swam past him. "Look out, here comes the shark!" they called.

Sandy just had time to hide inside an empty giant clam shell before the shark spotted him.

"You'll have to come out sooner or later," the shark snarled threateningly. Poor Sandy felt very frightened.

Sandy suddenly realized he
was starving. Then he remembered Marina's biscuits,
which he ate straight away. After that he felt a bit
better - but the shark was still circling above.

Suddenly a gleaming white dolphin came flashing
through the water. It was Silverfin. He made straight
for the shark, followed by many other dolphins.
The shark realized he was outnumbered, so
he sped away. Sandy crept out of his
clam shell and gratefully climbed onto
Silverfin's back. Then Silverfin carried
him swiftly to the city of the
mer-people.

Before long, Sandy was telling the mer-people about what had happened to Marina. It turned out that she was a mermaid princess, the youngest daughter of the king. "Take us to her," said the king, so Sandy proudly led the way, on Silverfin, with the mer-king and Marina's sisters and brothers following on their dolphins.

At last they came to Sandy's little boat. He clambered aboard it and carefully steered it between the jagged pieces of coral till he reached the shore. There he found Marina anxiously looking out to sea. He told her that her family was waiting for her beyond the reef.

"But how can I reach them?" she cried. "The coral is so sharp."

Just then, Jon and Wendy came running down. They had seen Sandy returning in his boat. "I'll carry Marina out to where the water is deep enough for her to swim safely," Jon said.

Wendy stood on the beach with Sandy and watched as
Jon carried Marina out over the coral. When they had
gone beyond the reef Marina said, "Thank you so
much. You've all been so kind to me." Then she
slipped from Jon's arms. With a splash of her
gleaming tail she was on her way.

Marina joyfully greeted her beloved dolphin Silverfin
and was soon surrounded by her family and friends. It
was a sight that Jon and Wendy would never forget.

Next morning, when Sandy pushed his cart along the tide-line as usual, he was overjoyed to find a thank-you gift from the mer-people.

It was a chest full of brightly colored jewels! So now Sandy's castle really sparkles in the sunshine-just as he had always dreamed it would.

THE SEVENTH UNICORN

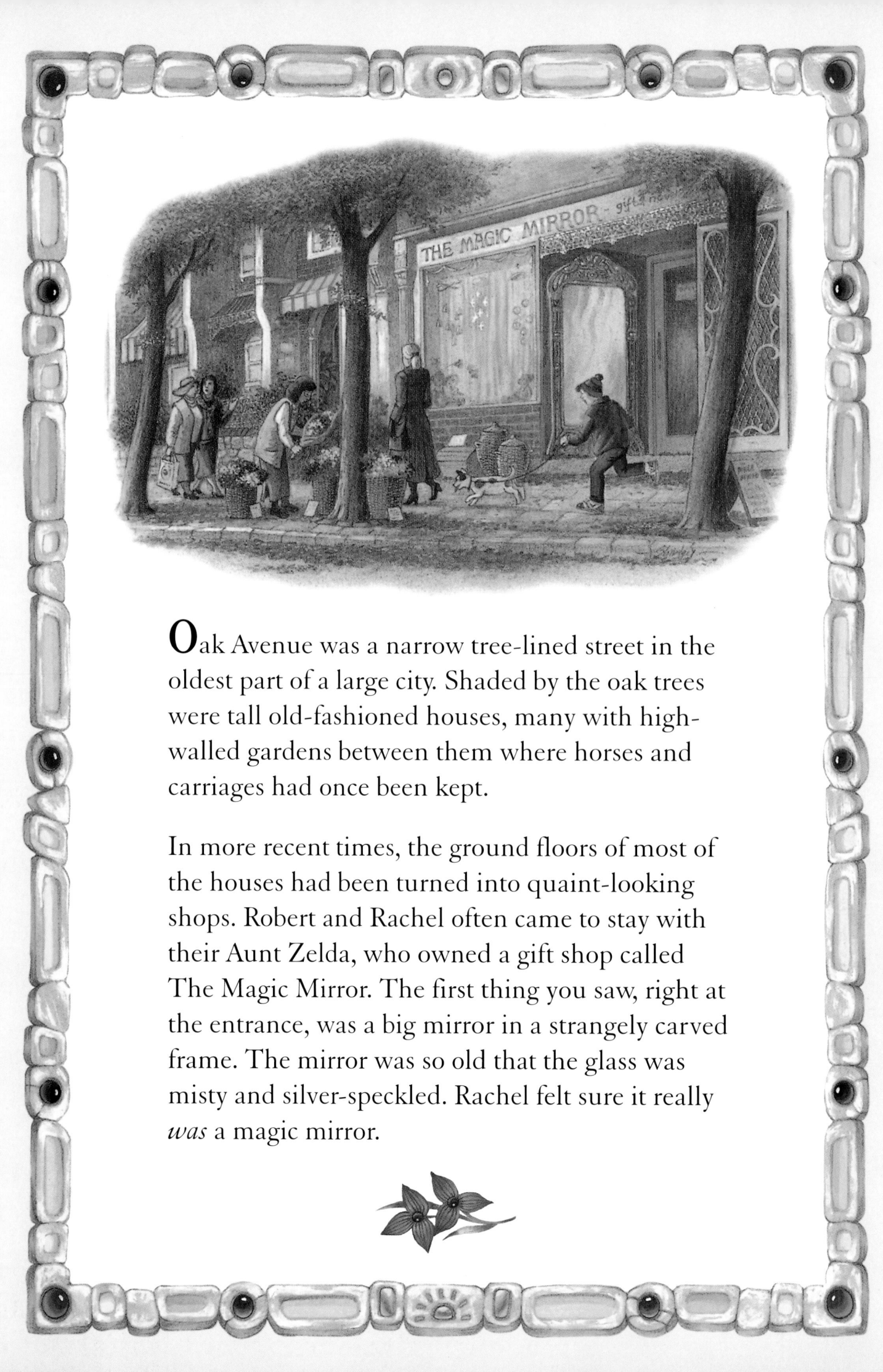

Oak Avenue was a narrow tree-lined street in the oldest part of a large city. Shaded by the oak trees were tall old-fashioned houses, many with high-walled gardens between them where horses and carriages had once been kept.

In more recent times, the ground floors of most of the houses had been turned into quaint-looking shops. Robert and Rachel often came to stay with their Aunt Zelda, who owned a gift shop called The Magic Mirror. The first thing you saw, right at the entrance, was a big mirror in a strangely carved frame. The mirror was so old that the glass was misty and silver-speckled. Rachel felt sure it really *was* a magic mirror.

"If you gaze into it for a long time you begin to see a beautiful world in there, behind the silver speckles," she said. Robert just laughed, but Aunt Zelda said, "You might see it more clearly if you gave the mirror a good polish."

So early next morning, before anyone was about, the children polished the mirror. Robert was impatient to go to the park at the end of the street to try out a new giant slide. As soon as they'd finished cleaning the mirror he ran off. Rachel was about to join him when a sudden movement made her glance back at the mirror.

Imagine her amazement when she saw a little pearl-white horse leap from the mirror in a swirl of stardust, and trot swiftly away between the trees. "A unicorn!" she whispered. "I'm sure it was a real live unicorn." Rachel ran to catch up to Robert.

"Oh, come on, Rachel," he said. "First a magic mirror and now a unicorn!" With that he dashed into a corner store to buy a bag of his favorite barley sugar twists.

"I really *did* see a unicorn," Rachel thought crossly to herself as she waited outside.

But when Robert reappeared and gave her some barley sugar she stopped feeling annoyed with him, and the two raced off to the park. The giant slide was such fun that Rachel almost forgot about what she had seen until...

...the little white unicorn trotted into view! His horn and hooves were golden and stardust glittered in his mane and tail. He came right up to the children, as if he wanted to play.

"What did I tell you?" Rachel whispered. "Isn't he beautiful!"

"Yes! And he absolutely loves barley sugar!" laughed Robert.

The honking of a distant car-horn startled the unicorn and he suddenly wheeled in a cloud of stardust and galloped away, his golden hooves silent on the autumn leaves.

"Let's go back and tell Aunt Zelda that her mirror really *is* magic!" said Rachel. So the children hurried back along Oak Avenue, but this time on the other side. As they were passing the high-walled yard next to The Wizard's Castle, an antique shop, Robert stopped suddenly.

"What is it?" asked Rachel. Without replying, Robert scrambledup the nearest oak tree and peered over the wall. "Rachel," he called down softly. "There are six more unicorns in there. They're all tied up, and they look very unhappy."

"Come down quickly!" hissed Rachel. "Someone's coming!" Down slid Robert, just in time.

A man had unlocked the shop door and was carrying out a strange assortment of antiques to arrange on the pavement outside. He wore a wizard's pointed hat with the name of his shop on it, and a cloak sewn with stars, so that he looked just like a real wizard. When he went back into the shop the children sped past and up the avenue towards Aunt Zelda's gift shop.

The children were almost at Aunt Zelda's shop when the seventh unicorn cantered past. Right before their eyes, he leapt back into the mirror.

"Come on!" cried Robert. "Follow him!" Despite his sister's protest, Robert pulled her with him into the mirror, and they went through the glass as if it were water.

On the other side of the
mirror Rachel's nervousness
faded as she saw they
had entered a beautiful
land, strangely shadowed
at the edges but filled
with jeweled flowers
and grasses.

"Welcome to Arcadia," said a soft voice
behind them. Rachel and Robert turned
and saw a group of beautiful children.
"Or welcome to what is left of Arcadia,"
said their leader. "For see how on every
side a shadow creeps to destroy our
lovely world."

Rachel and Robert looked where the girl pointed. They realized that what they had thought was a shadow was a really a creeping fog which had withered flowers and trees where it touched them.

"An evil wizard discovered the spell to open a door into our world," continued the young Arcadian leader. "Each day he entered thourgh the magic mirror, bound a unicorn with a magic halter and led it away. When he steals our last unicorn, Arcadia will be destroyed - only the power of seven unicorns keeps our world whole and well. We sent our seventh unicorn through the mirror to seek out the other six, but he couldn't find them."

Rachel and Robert looked at each other. *They* knew where the missing unicorns were. The wizard must have entered the magic mirror while Aunt Zelda was at the back of the shop.

The children quickly jumped through the magic mirror into the shop. Excitedly they told their amazed aunt all that had happened.

"We must work out a plan to rescue the other unicorns," she said, once she had recovered from her suprise. "We'll have to start very early in the morning before the wizard is out of bed - and we'll need a big bag of barley sugar!"

Next morning at sunrise, while Aunt Zelda guarded the magic mirror doorway, Rachel and Robert ran down Oak Avenue. Rachel kept a lookout for the wizard while Robert climbed over the wall to where the unicorns huddled miserably together.
He quietly unbolted the big gate and pulled off the magic halters, one by one. The six unicorns silently trotted out into the street, where Rachel gave them each some barley sugar. Soon the two children were running full speed up the avenue with the hungry unicorns following close behind.

Aunt Zelda was anxiously waiting outside her gift shop, ready to guide the unicorns back to Arcadia. Rachel leapt through the mirror, ahead of the unicorns, and threw handfuls of barley sugar among the jeweled flowers. The six unicorns followed her back into their own world, and began to crunch the barley sugar.

Next came Robert and Aunt Zelda. With cries of joy the Arcadians came running to hug and pet their unicorns, all seven together again at last. Then, golden light filled the land and the dark shadows were driven away.

For a moment they stood watching,
then Aunt Zelda drew the children
back to their own world...

... only to come face to face with the furious wizard!

"Let me pass!" he thundered. "I need the power of the unicorns to be the greatest wizard in the world."

Aunt Zelda quickly snatched up a heavy candlestick and shattered the mirror!

"The door is closed now," she said. "Arcadia is safe from you forever!"

The wizard scowled horribly, then stamped back to his antique shop and slammed the door.

Aunt Zelda and the children were overjoyed that
they had saved Arcadia from the wizard. They knew
they would never forget that beautiful world as long
as they lived. The ornate mirror frame was soon
fitted with a new glass, and although it was no
longer a doorway into another world, Rachel and
Robert often gazed into it. Sometimes they could
just make out a shimmering pearly form. They were
sure it was a unicorn looking out at them - perhaps
he was thinking about barley sugar!

The Five Mile Press

The Five Mile Press Pty Ltd
950 Stud Road, Rowville
Victoria 3178 Australia
Email: publishing@fivemile.com.au
Website: www.fivemile.com.au

First published 2002
Reprinted 2004 (three times), 2005

Copyright © Marbit Pty Ltd
www.shirleybarbers.com
Text and illustrations by Shirley Barber
CD produced by Stephanie Mann and Spoken Word Productions
This collection © The Five Mile Press Pty Ltd

Printed in China

National Library of Australia
Cataloguing-in-Publication data
Barber, Shirley
Shirley Barber's fairy stories.
For children.
ISBN 1 86503 779 6
1. Fairies - Juvenile fiction. I. Title. II. Title: Fairy Stories
A823.3